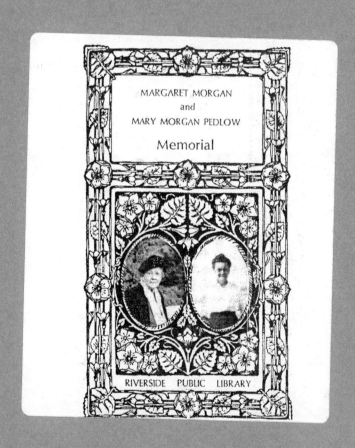

THE NEW BUNGALOW KITCHEN

THE NEW BUNGALOW
KITCHEN

PETER LaBAU

Photography by Marco Prozzo

The Taunton Press

T The Taunton Press

The Taunton Press, Inc., 63 South Main Street,
PO Box 5506, Newtown, CT 06470-5506
e-mail: tp@taunton.com

Editors: Pamela Thomas and Erica Sanders-Foege
Jacket/Cover design: Renato Stanisic
Interior design: Jeannet Leendertse
Layout: Jeannet Leendertse and Carol Petro
Illustrator: Scott Bricher
Photographer: Marco Prozzo

Library of Congress Cataloging-in-Publication Data

LaBau, Peter.
  The new bungalow kitchen / Peter LaBau.
     p. cm.
  ISBN-13: 978-1-56158-862-6
  ISBN-10: 1-56158-862-8
  1. Kitchens. 2. Kitchens--Remodeling. 3. Interior decoration. 4. Bungalows--United States.
5. Arts and crafts movement--Influence. I. Title.

NK2117.K5L33 2007
747.7'97--dc22

                                        2006024699

Printed in Singapore
10 9 8 7 6 5 4 3 2 1

The following manufacturers/names appearing in *The New Bungalow Kitchen* are trademarks: Amana®, Ann Sacks Tile®, Armstrong® Marmorette, Asko® Blanco Sinks®, Bosch®, The Bungalow Company℠, Chicago Faucet®, Congoleum Company®, Corian®, Dacor®, DCS®, Ellkay®, Enclume® from Sur La Table℠, Fisher & Paykel®, Forbo®, Forecast℠, Frigidaire®, General Electric®, GE Monogram®, GE Profile®, Genesis Architecture, LLC℠, Grohe®, Hafele®, Halo®, Hera®, Home Depot®, JennAir®, Juno®, Kenmore®, Kichler®, KitchenAid®, Kohler®, li'l Wok from Tech Lighting℠, Loewen®, Magic Chef®, Marvin®, Maytag®, Miele®, Mission Tile West®, Moen®, Montgomery Ward℠, Newport Brass®, Pozzi®, Price Pfister®, Reggio Registers®, Rejuvination, Inc.®, Restoration Hardware℠, Rohl®, Royal Window Company®, Runtal®, Seagull®, Sears®, Shaw®, Simpson®, SubZero®, Tech Lighting℠, Thermador®, Venmar℠, Viking®, Von Morris Corporation®, Wedgewood®, Westinghouse®, Whirlpool®, Whitehaus®, Wolf®

To my parents, David and Gretchen LaBau, for giving me the tools to design and build my dreams.

Acknowledgments

This book wouldn't have come to be without my introduction to Taunton Press by Treena Crochet, so thanks, Treena! And to editor Erica Sanders-Foege at The Taunton Press who came up with the topic for the book, which fits right into my passion for the design, restoration, and construction of historic and traditional American houses. Thanks to everyone else I worked with at Taunton: Peter Chapman, Robyn Doyon-Aitken, Wendi Mijal, and Katie Benoit. Also, a big thanks to Pam Thomas, who helped greatly with the editing of the book.

Thanks to photographer Marco Prozzo, who tirelessly traveled by car from Seattle to Maine, and then all the way back to create the beautiful images. We had a lot of fun getting to know each other, and working through how to best render the wonderful kitchens in the book.

Thanks to all the architects featured in the book, and to the homeowners who graciously made their homes available to us.

And last but not least, a humble thanks to all the known and unknown designers and builders of the thousands of Bungalow style-houses in this country. These houses set a high water mark for design, craft, affordability, and comfort that has yet to be equaled.

CONTENTS

INTRODUCTION

I can't begin to think of how many old houses I have been in over the course of the last 25 years, which was my tenure as the president and co-founder of The Classic Group, Inc., an architecture, interior design, and construction company in the Boston area. The company was born out of my belief in the practical and respectful integration of design and its execution—in other words, living design—and out of my love for historic and traditional American architecture.

As it was in my company, writing *The New Bungalow Kitchen* gave me an opportunity to bring together history and design as they pertain to Bungalow-style kitchens. And it gave me the opportunity to set down on the page some of what years of working on historical and traditional-style homes had taught me. Having just moved on from running the firm, I was eager to explore the popular Bungalow aesthetic, a period style that's beloved for its craftsmanship, richness of detail, and flexiblility. Of the many historical styles, it's perhaps the most easily adapted to the way we live today, which is one of the reasons why it's so appealing to me.

The New Bungalow Style

Clearly, I'm not the only one inspired by the Bungalow aesthetic. What continually fascinated me in the writing process was how architects, kitchen designers, and homeowners had interpreted the style. Not all the kitchens in the book are located in Bungalow or even Arts and Crafts style homes, nor are all the kitchens original to the homes. Some are brand new; a few are barely-renovated originals. And because I have an idea about the style, I've included one of my firm's projects (see p. 162). No other book has attempted to show how the Bungalow aesthetic can be interpreted in this most hardworking room of the house until *The New Bungalow Kitchen*. From the 17 beautifully-crafted kitchens photographed herein, a new definition has emerged.

It was important to me to express how I would work through the creation of a Bungalow-style kitchen in this book just the way I would with one of my clients. After so many years, I have developed an instinct for guiding people through the process. For example, first you must understand the historical context of the space you are endeavoring to improve. Then you must follow a series of logical steps for making it over in a new and functional space that fits your lifestyle. A newly constructed house—and its kitchen—that is styled on an older precedent is much the same.

This book is meant to inform you about the Bungalow style and its Arts and Crafts origins, and to help you to take certain liberties within the language of the style. In it, you'll learn the basics of Bungalow-style kitchens and their place in history. Layout strategies, discussed in Chapter Two, are at the heart of any renovation or new-build. I focus on how to treat walls, windows, floors and ceilings in Chapter Three. Cabinetry and storage—both major considerations for any kitchen but especially important to the Bungalow style which is virtually built on the idea of craftsmanship—are the main topic. "The Working Kitchen" or Chapter Five examines appliances that deliver convenience, and the final chapter explains how to apply lighting and hardware.

I know from my own use of many home design books by The Taunton Press that whether they are read cover to cover by a homeowner, or only used as a picture source book by a design professional, a good, logical framework is essential to their value. I hope you'll find this to be the case with *The New Bungalow Kitchen*, and that regardless of whether you are a homeowner or design professional, you will find this book a valuable part of your library.

Today, the kitchen is where we gather, we eat, and we work in our homes. To create one that reflects the beauty and history of the Bungalow is a true accomplishment. It's my hope that my book gives you the tools you need to get started on this rewarding journey.

—Peter LaBau

1 | THE ALLURE OF THE BUNGALOW KITCHEN

From their inception more than 100 years ago, Bungalow houses were specifically designed to integrate beauty with practicality, warmth with efficiency. Strongly influenced by the Arts and Crafts movement of the late 19th century, original Bungalows were small jewels that allowed their inhabitants to live easily and openly in lovely, comfortable homes. The Bungalow style has made a major comeback over the last decade, both in the restoration and renovation of old Bungalow houses and in the design and building of new ones. It's no wonder that the Bungalow style is enjoying a rebirth. And nowhere is that rebirth more welcome or exquisitely played out than in the new Bungalow-style kitchen.

This new kitchen in a 1920s Bungalow references the past with its dark wood and tile and linoleum flooring but includes many features that did not exist during the original Bungalow era, such as recessed lighting. Bungalow-style kitchens take the best attributes of the old kitchens and seamlessly blend them with the modern to create something entirely new.

Wide front porches were a hallmark of the Bungalow style. As with this 1913 Craftsman Bungalow, the front porch served as an "outdoor" room. To form the porch, the roof extended over the house and was supported by brick pillars. For privacy, homeowners often planted shrubbery or climbing plants on the sides of their porches.

The *New* Bungalow Kitchen

The way most of us live with—and in—our kitchens today is fundamentally different than how the original occupants of Bungalows lived a century ago. Back then, the kitchen was an austere, functional room where food was stored and prepared and dishes were washed. The kitchen, even in Bungalows where rooms flowed more openly from one to the other, was relegated to the back of the house, often cut off by a door.

For most of us today, the kitchen is the "heart of the home," not a space separated off. Most of spend more time in our kitchens than anywhere else in our homes, and this fact seems to be true whether we are young couples starting out; families with several children tramping in and out; retirees, scaling down; or singles of any age.

No matter our age or situation, we want all the benefits of the 21st-century technology, including state-of-the-art stoves, refrigerators, microwave ovens, not to mention computers, television sets, and media centers, all of which in recent years have made their way into the American kitchen. We also need to accommodate our 21st-century lifestyles, which often include more informal dining (or, unfortunately, dining-on-the-run) and entertaining. This means that we now need to incorporate the kitchen into what we now call "the family room," which, itself, often includes an informal dining area.

WHAT IS "BUNGALOW STYLE"?

Although the Bungalow style has infinite variations, it possesses a number of characteristics that are quickly recognizable and are useful to keep in mind when thinking about creating a new Bungalow-style kitchen. Specifically, Bungalow style refers to a type of small (usually one-story) house built in the United States between 1900 and 1940. Bungalows almost always featured large, deep front porches that often functioned as outdoor rooms or easy indoor-outdoor extensions of the house. And bungalows also often had many windows.

The interior style was borne of the Arts and Crafts movement, popular in England and the United States in the late 19th century. Typical elements included pronounced wood trim around windows, doorways, ceiling moldings and baseboards; hardwood floors; built-in furniture such as window seats, china cabinets, and bookshelves; stained-glass decorative windows and doors; tilework; and a subdued earth-tone color palette in its decoration.

In a marked break from their Victorian predecessors, the rooms were open and flowed easily one to the next. The Bungalow style evoked a feeling of warmth and comfort, yet, at the same time, managed to be functional and efficient.

This kitchen is a modern invention that still fits comfortably within an original California Bungalow. The design features, such as the heavy wood trim and the period-style hanging lamp, were greatly influenced by the rest of the house and have been incorporated into this new kitchen to feel as if they were always there.

The kitchen is part of a late 19th-century house, which is not one style or another—not Victorian yet not of the 20th century. Subtle Arts and Crafts touches, like open shelving, wainscoting, built-in cabinets, and a pale pastel color scheme, make this a perfect new Bungalow kitchen.

BUNGALOW STYLE

HALLMARKS OF THE NEW BUNGALOW KITCHEN

The Bungalow style, with its warmth, comfort, beauty, and inherent efficiency, is a natural option for kitchen decoration. Of course, if you live in a Bungalow or Arts and Crafts-style house, the choice is obvious. However, regardless of the style, size, or age of your house, a Bungalow-style kitchen, especially updated to suit the needs of our 21st-century lifestyles, is always appropriate. The new Bungalow kitchen:

- reflects the style of American Bungalow houses built between 1900 and 1940
- lavishly uses warm Arts and Crafts-style woodwork and metalwork in cabinetry, islands, and other kitchen furniture
- employs original (or reproduction) early 20th-century window treatments, flooring materials (linoleum), lighting fixtures, hardware (faucets; sinks), cabinetry, and other kitchen furnishings
- seamlessly links the 21st-century family room and informal dining areas, as well as state-of-the-art modern appliances, with the heart of an early 20th-century-style kitchen

At the same time, we want our kitchens to offer many of the same basic elements that draw us to Bungalow-style houses as a whole—the warm and welcoming atmosphere; the cozy, comfortable scale; and the simple, honest detail of the woodwork and other decorative elements.

Just because a Bungalow kitchen might not have contained all these elements originally, there's no reason why we can't combine them in a sensitive and informed manner in a 21st-century kitchen. For example, the "unfitted" look of the cabinetry—or cabinetry that was largely furniture—in the early Bungalows can actually be used to great effect in a contemporary Bungalow kitchen when it's properly influenced by the fancy woodwork of the formal rooms, particularly when the kitchen is made to open directly into these spaces.

Bungalow Houses, American Style

Of all the styles of American architecture, the early 20th-century Bungalow is known for its warmth and quality construction. The originals were built at a time when the love of craft was at its height, and the availability of quality materials and the tools and technology to assemble them were at a zenith.

The Bungalow style in the United States got its start on the West Coast and spread eastward, the first style of American architecture to do so. This classic California Bungalow, built in Palo Alto around 1918, is typical of the thousands that were constructed across the country in the early 20th century. The second story was not part of the original house but works with it seamlessly

Bungalows began to show up in the United States around 1880, first appearing in California and the Pacific Northwest. (The Bungalow was the first style of architecture to start on the West Coast of the United States and make its way east.) The warm climate of California was a perfect place for the style to take root, where its wide porches offered a cool respite from the sun.

Most American Bungalows had deep, inviting porches and somewhat formal front doors that led to cozy interiors. Some Bungalows had tiny entry vestibules, while others had large front porches that led directly into the living room. Although the houses were typically small, the rooms flowed from one to the next in an open, almost breezy way, making the house seem larger than it often was.

More than any other factor, Bungalows were strongly influenced by the Arts and Crafts movement (often called the Craftsman movement in the United States) of the late 19th century. Lavish houses in the Arts and Crafts style were being built across the country, including the Frank Lloyd Wright's Prairie style houses in the Midwest and Mission-style houses of the Southwest. The Bungalow-style houses were essentially somewhat smaller versions of Arts and Crafts houses.

THE ARTS AND CRAFTS MOVEMENT

BUNGALOW STYLE

The Arts and Crafts movement from England provided the framework and the momentum for the development of the American Bungalow and the Bungalow style. The Arts and Crafts style, made famous by the English designer William Morris, was in vogue in the latter half of the 19th century. By the early 20th century, American designers and architects influenced by the movement, notably Frank Lloyd Wright (Prairie style), Gustav Stickley (Craftsman style), and Charles and Henry Greene (Mission style), began to have a strong influence on the look of American houses and their interiors. Although the styles varied, often according to region, they shared many unifying features, all of which eventually evolved into the Bungalow style.

Most Arts and Crafts houses were small, yet open and airy. They featured a lavish use of natural wood, metal, stone, tile, and glass, inside and out, all with

meticulous attention to detail. The architecture and decoration focused on a strategic arrangement of rooms, windows, and doors, as well as through use of built-in furniture. The ultimate goal was integrate beauty and practicality in a modern, healthy, and efficient way.

Art-glass windows and cabinet fronts, oak woodwork and trim, and plank floors are all hallmarks of the Arts and Crafts-style interior. Here, the materials present a pleasing richness of texture.

Built-in furniture, such as window seats, breakfast nooks, shelving, and other snug places, is typical of the Bungalow style. This cozy built-in arrangement, part of a new Bungalow-style kitchen, allows for comfortable seating without sacrificing useful drawer space.

However, they incorporated the exquisite characteristic details such as tile, glass, metalwork, and especially dark, rich woodwork throughout the interior. The color palette featured earthy, neutral tones—dark reds, golds, greens, and browns.

A Departure from the Victorian

These houses were a major departure from the large-scaled houses of the late Victorian period and responded to the need of many middle-class Americans for a simpler, less expensive, and more efficient way of living. In the early 1900s, more and more people were moving from the hinterlands or from foreign countries, especially European countries, to urban areas to take advantage of employment opportunities in factories and other businesses. A simple Bungalow was an easy, and often economical, choice for a home for this increasingly mobile population.

Also, new attitudes toward a woman's role in society and the rapidly advancing technology freed homemakers from chores that had formerly consumed a woman's every waking moment. The small size of most Bungalows meant the house itself took less time to care for, which allowed for more time away from home, both to take advantage of the healthful outdoors (a new, and popular, concept) and to be involved in civic, religious, and other activities outside the home. In addition, a Bungalow required less furniture, not only because it was smaller but also because the Bungalow style made use of built-in furniture wherever it could, creating even more space.

The wide, sheltering porches that exemplify the Bungalow encouraged homeowners to spend more time in the open air, just sitting or entertaining on their porches. Stuffy, indoor Victorian activities quickly gave way to time spent outside. In fact, some of furniture magnate Gustav Stickley's popular Craftsman creations featured outdoor dining areas.

The Rise and Fall of the American Bungalow

The story of American Bungalows, and therefore of American Bungalow kitchens, falls naturally into two periods: the years leading up to and including World War I (about 1900 to 1920), and the two decades that follow, the 1920s, which were boom years, and the 1930s, which were economically devastating.

The years 1900 to 1920 define the period when "pure"—or original—Bungalow designs held sway. Built before and during the First World War, these houses can be called "Prewar Bungalows." It was during this time that the building of Bungalows boomed in the United States, not only

A tiny Arts and Crafts-style china cabinet, built into the corner of a breakfast room, provides a surprising amount of storage while not taking up much space.

Putting the "Kit" Back in Kitchen

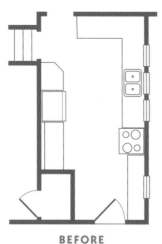

BEFORE

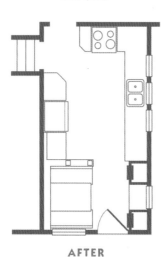

AFTER

From the turn of the 20th century until the late 1920s, Sears, Roebuck supplied economical, prebuilt houses in kit form to thousands of enthusiastic homeowners from coast to coast. These charming houses frequently cropped up in new "planned" suburban areas adjacent to larger cities, especially in the Midwest, like this 1916 house in Minneapolis. Built from "The Ashmore" design (dubbed the "aristocrat of Bungalows"), the original floor plans for this house were easy to find through old Sears catalogs and reprints. With a reprint in hand of an advertisement showing the original floor plan, the owner of this house worked with her architect to create a new Bungalow kitchen, making just a few small, respectful changes.

This particular kitchen had been remodeled several times since 1916, but the original floor plan revealed the logic of the initial kitchen plan arrangement. For the new kitchen, the owner decided to incorporate a former small back porch (that most likely housed the icebox) to make more room for a handsome entryway and mudroom. By taking a small amount of space from a large bedroom closet that backed up to the kitchen, a new, expanded breakfast nook was formed from an older, cramped "breakfast alcove" layout.

The old porch space was not missed at all, especially since a larger version was constructed just outside what is now the back door into the kitchen. The space taken from the adjacent bedroom closet was hardly noticed, while the benefit to the kitchen was enormous.

The original owners of this 1913 Bungalow would hardly know their kitchen. By combining characteristic elements (a worktable; white tiles; an old-fashioned apron sink; period-style light fixtures; warm wood cabinetry and trim including a picture rail) with state-of-the-art appliances, the current owners have evoked the comfort of the old Bungalow style with the elegance of the new.

in the West but also across the country, especially in the burgeoning suburbs of Chicago and other Midwestern cities.

Bungalows continued to be popular during the 1920s and 1930s and were built by the thousands. These houses, from 1921 through the late 1930s, are known as "Postwar Bungalows." While the Prewar Bungalows looked very similar regardless of where they were built, Postwar Bungalows came in a variety of styles to better accommodate different climates as well as other architectural influences that were developing at the time.

By the end of the 1930s, the Bungalow style had not only started to fade from popular taste, but it also began have a derogatory connotation. While many original American Bungalows were large, lavish, and beautifully designed, the term "bungalow" came to imply a small, mass-produced house. As with all trends, new ideas replaced the old, and, by the eve of World War II, architects and builders, in order to serve popular taste, had virtually abandoned the Bungalow style.

The Prewar Bungalow Kitchen: 1900 to 1920

Original Bungalow kitchens, built between 1900 and 1920, were isolated and spare by today's standards. The first bugaboo for owners of these older kitchens is that, in addition to being relatively small, they are usually located behind a closed door at the back of the house. Although there was access to the dining room (often through a pantry) as well as to the backyard (through a doorway and small porch), the kitchen still feels cut off from the rest of the house.

The second drawback is that the cabinetry and fixtures (not to mention the technologies) that filled them are archaic by today's standards. The working components of an original Bungalow kitchen included a sink area, a worktable (which sometimes also served as a dining table), a freestanding stove or range, an icebox, and wooden storage cabinets or open shelves. Cabinetry was rudimentary for the most part. Although the rest of an early traditional Bungalow featured beautiful dark woodwork, the kitchens were typically lighter, simpler affairs in order to better reflect light to make the space brighter and more cheerful.

The kitchens in early Bungalows were as different from their predecessors—the Colonial kitchen and the Victorian kitchen—as the rest of the house was. Early American kitchens were grimy places, but by the turn of the 20th century, the pendulum swung hard the other way.

As domestic researchers and social reformers provided models for clean, crisp kitchens that reflected new awareness of the relationship between

---

TIME GONE BY

Butler's Pantries
Originally the pantry (which derives from the Latin word, *panis*, or bread) was the place where the family's bread supply was stored. Over the centuries, the pantry evolved into the place where most of a household's dry goods were stored and organized. It became customary for a butler to take charge of a household's food supply (in the pantry), and as a result, the term "butler's pantry" was born.

KIT HOUSES

The Bungalow-style house was incredibly popular from the moment it first appeared, and fame was aided by companies like Sears® and Aladdin, which sold premanufactured Bungalow houses that could be easily shipped by rail anywhere in the country. Also, architectural plan firms like Radford and Bennett offered plan sets for Bungalow houses that could be executed by local builders. These companies made the Bungalow house affordable to people who might not have been able to own a house otherwise.

SEVEN ROOMS AND BATH

Honor Bilt

The Westly

No. P13085 "Already Cut" and Fitted

$2,614.00

THE WESTLY is a high grade two-story home, retaining the architectural beauty of a modern bungalow. Built everywhere. Every customer satisfied. Praiseworthy letters from Westly owners tell of the fine interior arrangement, beautiful woodwork, our approved "Honor Bilt" ready-cut system of construction, and of savings even as high as $1,500.00.

Exterior. Sided with narrow bevel clear cypress siding in first story; dormer, roof and second story covered with best grade of thick cedar shingles. Large front porch, 30 feet by 8 feet. Porch can be screened or glazed.

Can be built on a lot 35 feet wide

FIRST FLOOR PLAN

FIRST FLOOR

The Living Room. Size, 17 feet 8 inches by 13 feet 5 inches. An attractive feature is the open stairway that leads to the second floor. A coat closet with a mirror door is near the stairway. Furniture can be attractively arranged because of space. There are two windows at the side and one window at the front.

The Music Room. French doors connect with the living room. This music room is sometimes used for a bedroom instead. Size, 11 feet 2 inches by 9 feet 5 inches. Has a double window at the side and a high sash looking over the space for piano at the rear.

The Dining Room. A wide cased opening connects the living room and dining room. Size of dining room, 11 feet 2 inches by 12 feet 2 inches. Space for a complete dining set, including a buffet. Two side windows and one front window provide light and air.

The Kitchen. 11 feet 2 inches by 10 feet 8 inches. A swinging door connects with dining room. The space for sink, range, table and chair is laid out to save steps for the housewife. One side window and one rear window furnish light and cross ventilation. The pantry has five roomy shelves and a window.

A door from the kitchen opens into the rear porch, which has stairs to basement and to grade.

SECOND FLOOR

The Bedrooms. Stairs from the living room lead directly into a well lighted hall. This hall connects with the three bedrooms, bathroom and linen closet. The three bedrooms are all of good size. The front bedroom has a door to balcony. Each bedroom has two windows and a spacious clothes closet with a window. One bedroom has two clothes closets.

The Basement. Space for furnace, laundry and storage.

Height of Ceilings. First floor, 9 feet from floor to ceiling. Second floor, 8 feet 2 inches from floor to ceiling. Basement, 7 feet from floor to joists.

SECOND FLOOR PLAN

What Our Price Includes

At the price quoted we will furnish all the material to build this seven-room house, consisting of:

Lumber; Lath;
Roofing, Best Grade Clear Red Cedar Shingles;
Siding, Clear Cypress or Clear Red Cedar, Bevel;
Framing Lumber, No. 1 Quality Douglas Fir or Pacific Coast Hemlock;
Flooring, Clear Oak for Living Room, Dining Room and Music Room, Clear Maple for Kitchen, Pantry and Bathroom, Clear Douglas Fir or Pacific Coast Hemlock for Balance of Rooms;
Porch Flooring, Clear Edge Grain Fir;
Porch Ceiling, Clear Douglas Fir or Pacific Coast Hemlock;
Finishing Lumber;
High Grade Millwork (see pages 110 and 111);
Interior Doors, One-Panel Design for First Floor, and Two-Panel Design for Second Floor, All of Douglas Fir;
Trim, Beautiful Grain Douglas Fir or Yellow Pine;
Windows, California Clear White Pine;
Medicine Case;
Eaves Trough; Down Spout;
40-Lb. Building Paper; Sash Weights;
Chicago Design Hardware (see page 132);
Paint for Three Coats Outside Trim and Siding;
Stain for Two Brush Coats for Shingles on Gable Walls;
Shellac and Varnish for Interior Trim and Doors;
Shellac, Paste Filler and Floor Varnish for Oak and Maple Floors.
Complete Plans and Specifications.
We guarantee enough material to build this house. Price does not include cement, brick or plaster. See description of "Honor Bilt" Houses on pages 12 and 13.

OPTIONS

Sheet Plaster and Plaster Finish, to take the place of wood lath, $234.00 extra. See page 109.
Oriental Asphalt Shingles, for roof, guaranteed 17 years, instead of wood shingles, $36.00 extra.
Oak Doors and Trim for living room, dining room, also Oak Stairs, $130.00 extra.
Storm Doors and Windows, $100.00 extra.
Screen Doors and Windows, galvanized wire, $62.00 extra.
For prices of Plumbing, Heating, Wiring, Electric Fixtures and Shades see pages 130 and 131.

For Our Easy Payment Plan See Page 144

Part of a large 1930s Arts and Crafts-style house, this opulent Bungalow-style kitchen fits well within the kitchen's footprint. Original Bungalow kitchens were meant to be white and clean looking, and this new kitchen combines stark, white cabinetry and walls with warm wood touches to achieve a contemporary look that still evokes the past.

TIME GONE BY

Early Bungalow kitchens did not have the characteristic lush Arts and Crafts woodwork like the rest of the house. For reasons having to do with attitudes about hygiene, original Bungalow kitchens were stark, clean, functional, and usually white. Also, although the classic Bungalow was more or less open space (especially compared with its Victorian predecessor), the kitchen was closed off at the back of the house.

dirt and disease, every effort was made to use materials in the kitchen that were smooth and easy to clean. Wallpaper was banished because it was not considered sanitary, and kitchen walls were usually finished with either painted or tinted plaster, which was easy to wash. Wooden wainscoting that had been much a part of 19th-century Victorian kitchens was viewed as being a hiding place for pesky microbes, and so quickly became passé in early Bungalow kitchens.

Like the walls, ceilings were usually plain painted plaster or were covered with painted pressed-tin tiles. If budget allowed, floors were covered with ceramic tile, which gave the kitchens a more "laboratory" look than the cluttered appearance of the Victorian kitchen. Those who could not afford expensive ceramic tile could choose brightly colored linoleum floor covering (new at the time) or smooth, easy-to-clean tongue-and-

This circa 1920 Bungalow kitchen is humble in appearance yet provides the seeds for the more sophisticated look of today's Bungalow kitchen.

groove flooring in softwood species such as heart pine, fir, or southern yellow pine. Painted floor cloths were sometimes used as a colorful, easy-to-clean covering for these wood floors.

Early Kitchen Furniture

Cabinetry in the early Bungalow kitchen was freestanding, fairly primitive, and didn't display the wonderful woodwork that appeared in other parts of Bungalow-style houses. Typically, plain shelving or cupboards held pots, pans, dishes, and other supplies. A host of new "kitchen cabinets" such as those produced by the Hoosier Company, were a common sight in the first period and allowed for an efficient way to combine storage spaces and work surfaces. These were the predecessors of the modern "fitted," or site-built, kitchen cabinets that began to show up in the 1920s and 1930s.

The cookstoves were usually heavy, black iron devices that vented into a chimney and also provided the only source of heat for the kitchen. As water heaters came into being, they were located on metal stands next to the range so they could share the chimney. The icebox was almost always located in an alcove by the back door or sometimes out on the back porch to keep the iceman from tracking his muddy boots across the kitchen floor when he made his daily delivery of ice.

The Shock of Electricity

Although electric lighting was coming into use in many homes in the early 1900s, gas was still the lighting source in most of the early Bungalow kitchens. These lighting fixtures had a more primitive appearance than the ones that came later. Although gas was used for lighting, it is interesting to note that the use of gas as a cooking fuel didn't catch on for several more years; as a result, heavy, black coal- and wood-burning stoves were still central to the Bungalow kitchen.

Nevertheless, the use of electricity was quickly changing how people lived. By 1910, most cities had electricity, although most rural areas did

The Victorian-era butler's pantry was a forerunner of modern cabinetry. This pantry owes a debt of gratitude to that which came before it. Although the style is contemporary, the fine Arts and Crafts woodwork is certainly at home, helping to create a modern look that works well in a new Bungalow kitchen.

Linoleum was less expensive and easier to care for than wood, and came in a wide variety of colors and patterns in the early 1900s. Linoleum went out of style for decades, but, especially because of its eco-friendly qualities, it's back—and a perfect choice for any Bungalow kitchen.

New Nostalgia

It's sometimes difficult to see beyond what others have done in bad kitchen remodels. Luckily for the owner of this 1907 Memphis, Tennessee, Bungalow, his skills as an architect allowed him to see through walls lined with generic cabinetry, a dropped ceiling, and bad finishes to explore options for creating the right kitchen for his home.

The original kitchen was much smaller than the owner wanted. After creating a floor plan of the kitchen's existing footprint as well as the adjacent spaces, the architect immediately saw that by simply eliminating a large pantry at the rear of the kitchen, he would have a much more pleasing space. He also opted to expand "up," removing an ugly ceiling from an earlier remodel that stole almost 2 ft. of space from the height of the room.

Once the kitchen was stripped down to its bare bones, it evoked a strong sense of the house's early Bungalow style, and the architect went with that feeling of nostalgia. Instead of fitted cabinetry, he went with an old-fashioned furniture style but used it in a con-temporary way. An antique display case serves as a central kitchen island; old cabinets are combined with new ones for a less formal look; and a pale color palette is used on the walls and trim. Darker stained wood trim is used not only on the floor but also on the newly restored ceiling.

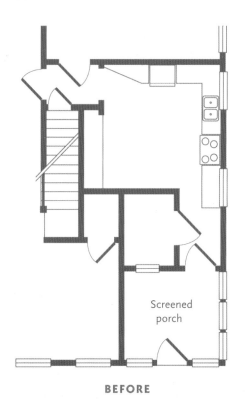

Screened porch

BEFORE

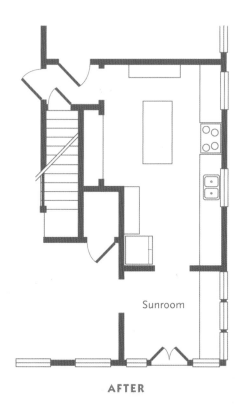

Sunroom

AFTER

In a renovated original Bungalow, antique lighting fixtures like this one help to seamlessly connect a new kitchen to an old house.

nor Bungalow dwellers fortunate enough to have electricity also had lighting fixtures that were designed to be consistent with the rugged, handmade look of the Craftsman style.

In its infancy, electricity wasn't imagined for use to power devices other than lights. Since lights were only used at night, the electric power plants of the time didn't provide electricity during the day. Manufacturers such as General Electric® and Westinghouse®, which produced early electric toasters, mixers, irons, dishwashers, fans, and other household appliances, were the ones that pressured the utility companies to provide power 24 hours a day.

The first electric refrigerators came on the market in 1917. In the years before electricity became the norm, iceboxes were fairly sophisticated, but with the invention of the electric refrigerator, iceboxes were rendered obsolete almost overnight.

BUNGALOW STYLE

MRS. FREDERICK, THE MARTHA STEWART OF HER DAY

Martha Stewart was not the first woman to build a business by promoting domesticity. Between 1912 and 1929, a Long Island housewife named Christine Frederick, who came to be known simply as Mrs. Frederick, developed a national reputation by advising women on how to be better homemakers. A popular lecturer and author of books and numerous magazine articles, Mrs. Frederick was an efficiency expert and disciple of scientific management, claiming that women should approach domestic work as a profession, that manufacturers should develop products to help the housewife, and that women should avidly buy and use them. She claimed responsibility for advocating raising the kitchen sink to make it easier for women to wash dishes. By promoting the application of technology in the name of greater household efficiency, Frederick endeavored to make housework more satisfying for middle-class housewives who no longer could rely on domestic servants to run their homes.

A period piece like this 1930s Magic Chef® gas range provides a beautiful anchoring presence in a new Bungalow kitchen. New gas valves and door gaskets allow this range to perform almost as well as the new ones.

The Postwar Bungalow Kitchen: 1921–1940

Bungalows remained a popular house style in the early 1920s but were experiencing increasing competition from the ever-popular Colonial, as well as the Tudor, Foursquare, Mediterranean, and other styles that were enjoying new life, retooled into small, comfortable, and affordable designs. The classic Bungalow style was also beginning to absorb other influences and didn't look quite so much like a direct descendent of the Arts and Crafts movement.

Nevertheless, in the Bungalow kitchens of the 1920s, built-in cabinetry became more popular than the earlier freestanding storage devices like the Hoosier. This meant that the kitchen cabinetry and the rest of the woodwork in the kitchen could take on an appearance more consistent with the rest of the woodwork in the formal rooms of the house. Cabinetry was also beginning to take up more space in the kitchen. Building-material catalogs of the time show built-in kitchen cabinetry that looks very similar to today's layouts.

By the 1920s, most Bungalows had hot and cold running water available throughout the house, so the tall hot-water heater that had once been located in the kitchen was now placed in the basement. The heavy, black cookstoves of the early 20th century were now being replaced by gas ranges (sometimes coated with colored enamel) with accurate thermostats, which meant stoves could be left unattended while meals cooked.

Electric lighting was now firmly established, but lighting fixtures in the kitchen, as elsewhere in Bungalows, were fewer, smaller, and produced much less light overall than we are used to today. The use of electric appliances, especially refrigerators and stoves, as well as many electric kitchen gadgets became more and more popular during the '20s and '30s. With no iceman tracking in dirt, the refrigerator could be moved closer into the working core of the kitchen, although out of force of habit, it often stood where the old icebox was once located.

Freestanding kitchen tables were formalized into breakfast nooks, an architectural element that was usually positioned next to an outside wall with a window to provide a sunny spot in the kitchen. Built-in cabinetry and other kitchen furniture helped to streamline the appearance of the kitchen overall. It is this crafted, economical approach intrinsic to the Craftsman Bungalow that we most closely associate with Bungalow style today.

By the 1930s, the overall Bungalow style was brighter and more airy than the dark-wood style that had predominated just a few years before. Here, a new kitchen, part of a 1930s Tudor-style house, blends the Bungalow and the Tudor styles.

Breakfast nooks were popular in Bungalow-style kitchens almost from the start. This lovingly renovated nook in a 1916 Sears "kit" Bungalow shows how the new Bungalow kitchen can incorporate all the warmth and whimsy of the old.

TIME GONE BY

Mail-order Catalogs

Throughout the 19th century, women had increasing access to information, tools, and technology that maximized their productivity in the kitchen. Rather than just sharing tips with neighbors, women entered a world of new ideas through magazines and books that specialized in recipes, home maintenance, and kitchen layout. After 1900, companies such as Sears and Montgomery Ward℠ supplied stoves, ranges, iceboxes, floor coverings, all manner of kitchen gadgets—virtually anything needed to modernize the kitchen.

This evolving aesthetic brought the kitchen more in line with the rest of the formal rooms of the first floor. And while the kitchen was always kept lighter than the rest of the house, by the 1930s, a more lively color palette was introduced. The black stove and white sink were replaced with cool, pastel colors, often mirrored by the linoleum on the floor and paint on the walls. By 1940, when Bungalow-style houses were going out of fashion, the kitchens had developed a characteristic look, especially with their fitted cabinetry, that would remain the convention for decades to come.

A Kitchen Style for Today

Our fast-paced contemporary lifestyles makes us yearn for the cozy comfort of the Bungalow aesthetic. At the same time, we use the home kitchen in much different ways than families did a century ago. Now we want our kitchens to belong to the rest of our living space, easily accessed, and part of the flow of the rest of the house. The trick is to blend all the kitchen equipment we have today with the period feel of the Bungalow style so that a brand-new kitchen looks like it was always there. After all, anyone can simply copy a museumlike setting, but making it livable by modern standards is the real challenge.

BUNGALOW STYLE

PLAYING A TIME MACHINE GAME

Most contemporary Bungalow owners face a conundrum when considering ways to make their kitchen work as a modern space. One way that I approach this problem with my clients is to play a "time machine" game.

We pretend that we are gathered around the kitchen table with the original architect and/or builder of the house in question. We provide our imaginary collaborator with some new demands on the kitchen space they designed decades before, along with a list of new technologies. We then ask our guest(s) to help us apply this new information in the redesign of our new kitchen. In short, we want to make the kitchen learn some new tricks but not to give up its inherent design aesthetic.

This is usually a step-by-step process. We look carefully at each element required for a new kitchen: the space it will encompass; the central core; the cabinetry; the appliances; and the lighting, hardware, and other finishing touches. Then we look at all of the elements of the old that we love so much and very carefully put them together.

A brand-new Bungalow kitchen is the heart of an entirely new Bungalow house. With its wood-faced island and matching cabinetry, simple wood-trimmed windows, dark tile, and stained floor, the kitchen is a clear descendent of the original Bungalows. Its airy openness makes it a perfect kitchen for our modern lifestyle.

2 | MAKING ROOM: RECONFIGURATIONS AND ADDITIONS

Kitchen design has come a long way since the turn of the 20th century when Bungalows first appeared on the scene. Today, in addition to coveting the latest stoves, refrigerators, and other appliances, most of us want our kitchens to "communicate" with the rest of the house, at least more than the original Bungalow kitchens did. Indeed, many of us yearn to have a kitchen that serves as the heart of our home, with a family room, an attractive yet informal dining area, and possibly even a super-convenient home office within steps of the space where food is prepared.

In a 1913 Bungalow, the sensitively updated kitchen has a worktable positioned characteristically in the center of the workspace. The Arts and Crafts-style cabinetry in natural finished oak reflects the original period style and adds a warmth that is enhanced by the strip flooring.

Happily, a Bungalow-style kitchen can be perfectly integrated into any house, regardless of whether it is an original Bungalow. Your house might be a Colonial saltbox, a Victorian manse, a 1950s ranch, or a new house of any style. As a designer, I've always made it my mission to create environments in old houses where new spaces coexist with the original parts in a harmonious fashion. At the same time, I believe older styles—in this case, the Bungalow style—can work beautifully in newer, or even brand-new, houses.

A newly renovated kitchen in an original 1910s California Bungalow was relocated from the middle to the rear of the house to better link the kitchen to the driveway and the backyard. Interior walls and doorways were moved to add space, and windows were added for better light and circulation—all without the need for an addition.

The kitchen is the culinary center of a brand-new house, further proof that you don't have to live in an original Bungalow to create the look and feel of an original Bungalow kitchen.

Setting a realistic budget

It's fun and useful to explore all the options when embarking on a kitchen renovation, but in the end for most of us, budget rules. There are two basic considerations: how much you can really afford to spend and how much it makes sense to spend, given your home's real value in the marketplace and its intrinsic value to you.

Most properties (or at least the type you are likely to own if you are considering a kitchen renovation) are going to appreciate over time, so the longer you keep them, the more they'll be worth when you want to sell. If you plan to stay in your house for a long time, investing a significant amount of money in a kitchen renovation and getting exactly what you want makes sense. However, if you plan to move within a few years, then you should play it more conservatively.

Also, if you just recently bought your house and paid top dollar, then you won't have much margin left to sink into the house. Still, kitchens are typically the best home-improvement investments, so you stand a better chance of recouping the costs for a thoughtful, well-executed kitchen renovation than putting in a swimming pool, for example.

Have a dialogue with a good local real estate agent about how much your house is currently worth and what it might be worth with a new kitchen. Once you have a handle on the amount of money it makes sense objectively to put into a kitchen renovation, balance this amount against your actual means. Now you have a realistic budget.

Next, talk with a few qualified builders to figure out how far you can go with your plans. Although builders generally have a better sense of true costs than architects, an architect can also provide lots of help for your renovation.

Creating a kitchen in a particular style depends to a large extent upon the design details, especially the cabinetry, lighting, and hardware. However, before we can begin to discuss design details, we need to make space for the kitchen itself, in this case, a *new* Bungalow-style kitchen, often including a family room or dining area, in an *old* Bungalow-style house. (If your house is not a Bungalow, don't worry; much of this basic information will still apply.)

First Thoughts: Three Basic Choices

If you're planning to update your existing kitchen in the Bungalow style, you'll approach the project in one of three ways. You can:

- work within the footprint of the original kitchen

- appropriate existing adjacent spaces, such as closets, hallways, or pantries

- build an addition

The most fundamental way to proceed is to work within the confines, or footprint, of the original kitchen. That is, you don't change the basic floor plan of the original kitchen; instead, you either gut it and start over or save parts of it and work around them.

If layout, budget, and time allow, then you can stretch out a little and start looking at appropriating spaces that are adjacent to the kitchen, such as closets, pantries, mudrooms, storage areas, or old stairways. With this approach, you might also consider moving interior walls and changing the location of exterior windows and doors.

Finally, if no real satisfaction can be found by either maintaining the original footprint or "stealing" adjacent spaces, then you can take the most ambitious approach and add on to your house. Working from this plan, your first step is to hire an architect. A good designer will integrate aspects of the original kitchen or surrounding areas to make the most of the added space. You may find that even a small addition, or "bump-out" as it is known, can add a delightful element to the appearance and usefulness of an older house.

Critical space for the kitchen was created by taking over a screened porch, which allowed for a breakfast room. Walls of windows allow the owners to bask in morning light as they linger over coffee and the paper.

Unless clients are convinced that they need an addition at the beginning of the design process, I always explore the less invasive renovation schemes first. Besides being more economical, these options allow more of the original design integrity of the house to remain. You'd be surprised what can be done with some creative thinking when working in old houses.

Sticking to the (Floor) Plan

Creating a new kitchen in the footprint of the old one is essentially a good way to go if you have few options either financially or logistically for boldly going where no one has gone before. Also, if you are basically happy with the locations of things in your kitchen but just want to renew them, of course, stick with the old layout.

Many Bungalows sit on small suburban lots that include driveways, yards, trees, garages, and other space grabbers, so planning a full addition is often simply not possible. Also, many owners of original bungalows want to maintain the beauty and simplicity of the original design of their house, both inside and out.

Finally, of course, there's the issue of cost, and keeping the renovation within the original floor plan of the kitchen will almost always be the most economical. Any change to windows or doors that affects the exterior of the house brings in another level of work and, consequently, expense. Making exterior wall changes can quickly lead to carpentry repairs and may even require repainting the entire outside of the house.

Getting in Touch with History

With Bungalows, it makes sense to try to understand how your kitchen was originally set up. Most kitchens in older Bungalows have been renovated at least once, and some may have been changed many times. Attitudes about how kitchens ought to work have changed over the years, and the solutions that have been implemented are not always good ones. If they were, you'd probably be reading recipes now instead of this book. Inexpensive older (and many newer) kitchen remodels often imposed generic solutions, such as poorly designed cabinetry that was insensitive to the style and integrity of the house. Returning to what might have been

A 1917 Midwestern Bungalow is characteristic of thousands of such charming houses built on small suburban lots. The owners chose to stay within the house's existing floor plan for their renovation, not only for budgetary reasons but also because an addition would not fit comfortably on their modest-size lot.

This classic Bungalow-style kitchen is an important part of a new Bungalow house, the plans for which were created by a firm that specializes in predesigned plan sets.

An eclectic look is perfectly in keeping with a Bungalow-style kitchen. In a 1917 Bungalow kitchen in Memphis, the cabinetry is freestanding and built-in, which creates a warm, casual cooking environment.

the original cabinet layout in your kitchen is a good place to start thinking about a new renovation. After all, it was built that way for a reason.

Many older Bungalows, especially those built before World War I, had cabinetry that was "unfitted." That is, the storage units and appliances, including Hoosiers, furniture-style cupboards, worktables, stoves, and iceboxes were freestanding. Using unfitted cabinetry can work beautifully, even today, especially when you must contend with existing window and door locations. Later, Bungalows featured fitted cabinets in the kitchen, but the woodwork was never as crafted as the woodwork throughout the rest of the house. In addition, appliances such as stoves and refrigerators, even as late as the 1930s, were much smaller than the ones we use today.

Making Basic Improvements

Often with only minor adjustments, the cabinetry layout in a Bungalow kitchen can be improved, even from the original. For example, in most Bungalows, cabinetry was lined up around the walls, and the center of

BUNGALOW BASICS

Digging up the past

Figuring out what your kitchen first looked like can be an enormous help when you are trying to come up with a new layout. Drawing a floor plan is the best way to re-create the past. Often the most revealing clues are on the ceiling of the basement under the kitchen. Newer floor framing can be seen juxtaposed to the old, and pipe, wire, and heating duct reroutes can be easily spotted.

In the kitchen, flooring patches are another giveaway that something was altered. These modifications are usually visible only after several layers of vinyl, linoleum, and other "added" floors have been taken up and the first flooring exposed. Wall changes will leave scars in the floor as well, indicating the locations of earlier walls. Interruptions or oddly located cut lines in baseboards or other wood trim can reveal that a door once existed or was moved.

Keep adding new archeological information into your floor plan. And if you are lucky, you might find an original set of drawings hidden in the basement or attic. A little research at the local historical society might also reveal that your house was a kit house or built from purchased plans, in which case you might be able to find your original floor plan online.

Small Changes That Make a Big Difference

One of the problems with original Bungalow layouts was that they isolated the kitchen at the back (or sometimes the side) of the house, usually behind a closed door. When original Bungalow houses were being designed in the early 20th century, it was the fashion to keep room functions discreet from one another, particularly in the case of kitchens, where noise, food preparation, cooking smells, and serving functions were not to be put on display for guests or even family members. The result was often dark kitchens and dining rooms that sometimes felt cramped and unfriendly.

This neat pass-through space between the kitchen and the dining area provides an ingenious solution to that problem. It was not an original feature of this 1913 Midwestern Bungalow; in fact, the original doorway to the kitchen was right in the middle of what is now the pass-through. In the 1950s, the door was moved to the left and the wall closed up so the stove could be located in that spot. At the same time, a much smaller pass-through was installed, essentially providing a "slot" in the wall to ease serving and add a little more light.

When the current owners, who are remarkably resourceful folks, began to consider their kitchen renovation, they decided that the existing appliances and cabinetry would remain where they were for several reasons. For starters, staying within the original kitchen's floor plan was much more economical, allowing the budget for the kitchen to be applied to fun stuff like new cabinets, appliances, and finishes. But more important, logically, there was no better place to put them, especially since the stairway to the second floor was in the back of the kitchen, and the kitchen needed to remain as open as possible.

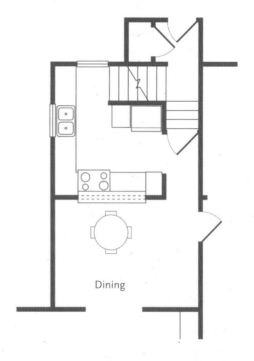

Dining

By making this pass-through taller and wider, the owners were able to visually open up the kitchen/dining space, creating more light and airiness, without adding so much as an inch to the footprint of the house. From the kitchen, the larger pass-through allows for a nice sight line into the dining room and through to the front door, while the half-wall establishes enough separation between the two spaces to preserve the original intent of the Bungalow. The bigger pass-through makes the kitchen and dining room feel more contemporary, but the beautiful use of wood trim and cabinetry places it firmly in its historic Bungalow style.

RAISING THE CEILING

One of the most often performed bogus modifications to early 20th-century Bungalow-era kitchens was to install a dropped ceiling. This was usually done because the original ceiling had begun to deteriorate or because it was easier to cover up wiring, plumbing, or heating ductwork across the old ceiling than it was to open up the old ceiling.

Depending on the situation, a ceiling might have been dropped anywhere from a few inches to a few feet below the original, causing the room to lose height, making the whole kitchen feel smaller and more claustrophobic than it actually is.

Particularly when you are considering doing simple renovation where no change is intended to the floor plan of your kitchen, returning the ceiling to its original height is a critical move. Removing a dropped ceiling may expose some things you will need to fix, but it's usually worth the effort. The added height will make an enormous difference in your new kitchen.

the kitchen was either left open or featured a kitchen table. In a Bungalow kitchen, this sort of arrangement is often able to accommodate a small island, which might include cabinets, a dishwasher, a sink, additional workspace, and even a casual place to sit. Appliances can be relocated, a sink can be moved to a window location, and cabinets can be changed, all within the original layout. Still, the most economical solution is to update the contents of the kitchen with only minor changes to the original layout.

The same idea applies to fundamental systems. As with any kitchen renovation, moving their locations, particularly plumbing, heating, and electrical devices, will ratchet up the costs dramatically. This is especially true with Bungalows because, if it's original, the plumbing should be replaced. Keeping pipes in their original locations allows the plumber to work with existing routes, saving reframing costs and work time.

On the other hand, Bungalows are modest in size, so like any old house, the plumbing was often grouped in one corner. Bathrooms were placed near kitchens so the plumbing could share the same stack or waste line. Unfortunately, this schematic doesn't necessarily answer our needs today for a supply line to the fridge for the icemaker, one to the island for the prep sink, or new lines for the sink that's been relocated across the room. And although this adds to the cost of your remodel, it's smart to do all the work at the same time.

The same holds true for electrical lines. Very old wiring, plugs, and other related systems and infrastructures should always be replaced, but moving their fundamental locations means additional cost. On the other hand, for that office niche carved out of a corner, it's nice to have a cable hookup or an outlet dedicated for the computer, so consider upgrading these functions at the same time you replace the old wiring.

Trading Spaces

If you are willing to make some bigger changes and are able to push beyond the boundaries of your present kitchen, then many more options open up. These choices are directly related to the kinds of spaces you can take over for new use in your kitchen.

The owner swapped out all the old cabinetry, appliances, and finishes in this early 20th-century kitchen for new. He designed and built the stained-glass windows to evoke the Arts and Crafts style of Frank Lloyd Wright.

Coming up with the plan

Regardless of whether you are building a new kitchen within its preexisting shell, breaking through to adjacent spaces, or creating an addition, I strongly recommend that you make a detailed floor plan of your existing kitchen. In fact, it's probably a good idea to make a drawing of the entire first floor of your house, even if you are projecting a simple renovation. Whether you carefully measure out your plan and put it on graph paper yourself or have it done for you by an architect or designer, your options for design won't really become obvious until you are, in effect, looking down from above. Then, you'll see how all appliances, windows, doorways, and adjacent spaces interact and how the rooms near your kitchen flow—or don't flow—from one to the other.

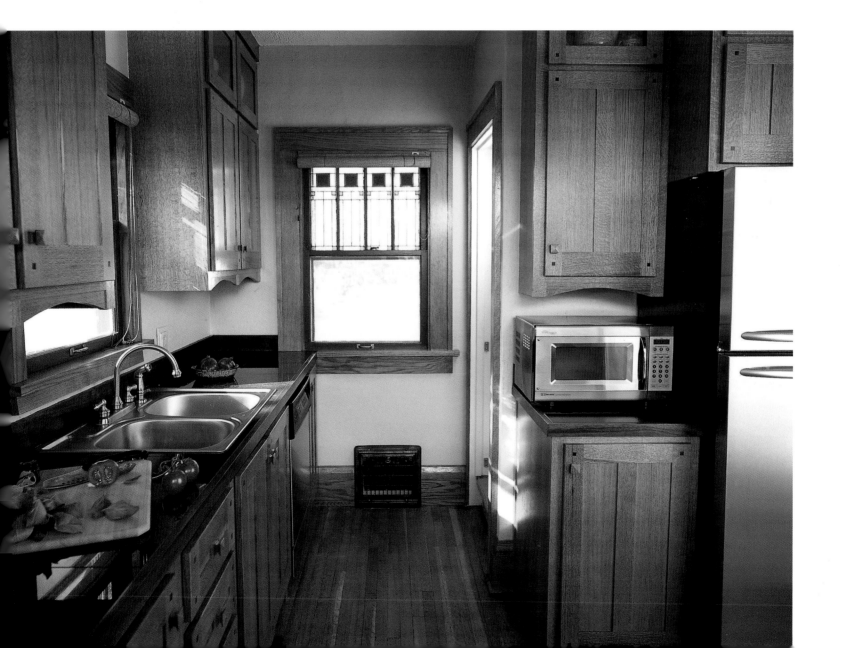

A nook tucked in among bookcases is characteristic of the early Bungalow period. Suitable for morning breakfast or evening supper, this lovely dining area can be easily reconfigured to accommodate more people.

Typical spaces that often can be reappropriated beyond the kitchen in a Bungalow are storage rooms, closets, pantries, service stairs, porches, mudrooms, and hallways. Sometimes even accessing portions of adjacent rooms, such as an end of a formal dining room that is rarely used, can net big gains without really affecting that room's function. Moving windows and relocating doorways can also result in surprising solutions to space problems. A common fix in the Bungalow kitchens I've designed is to move the door leading to the mudroom from the center of the wall to the corner in order to make wall space for a full run of cabinets. And often I like to replace full-height windows that may have looked out to the back porch with ones that fit above the 3-ft. counter height to create more workspace.

Before you start to howl at the possible loss of something as profound as a stairway or currently useful pantry space, remember that "back stairs" and "butler's pantries" reflect the way people lived in Bungalows at the

Celebrating rather than hiding quirks in a Bungalow kitchen can add so much to the finished look of a successful renovation. The plastered curve of the underside of a narrow servant's staircase adds a playful design aspect to a renovated pantry.

BUNGALOW BASICS

Doors and Doorways

Doors and doorways are terms that we use interchangeably, but we often confuse them. An opening between two rooms that is the size of a regular door but that has no door in it is, in fact, a "cased opening," whereas a "doorway" is actually a cased opening that is fitted with a hinged door.

Most cased openings in older Bungalows were fitted with doors even though one may not exist there now. Wider cased openings, such as between a dining room and a living room, might have framed a pair of doors or pocket doors that would slide out to screen one room from another.

It's usually easy to tell if a cased opening used to be a doorway. Just look carefully at the doorjambs for wooden patches where the old hinges used to sit. Unless a very skilled carpenter did the patching, you can always see a ghost of the old hinge through the paint or stain finish of the doorjamb.

Study the doorways and cased openings in your Bungalow. If you're a purist, you may want to add a long-lost door in an old-fashioned doorway. On the other hand, you may want to remove a door or two or widen an existing cased opening to make your old Bungalow kitchen more visually connected to the adjacent rooms.

FROM PORCH TO PANTRY

Old back porches are great targets for reuse and can often provide needed floor space for your kitchen renovation when they are opened up to the inside. But it's important to carefully evaluate the structure before you move ahead to incorporate the space into your new kitchen or family room. Porches were typically situated on brick or wood piers, which can be structurally shaky or inadequate to withstand the heavy load of a new addition. It's imperative for you to get a professional builder, architect, or structural engineer to inspect it.

Cracked or soggy supports under porches may need to be rebuilt. In this case, you may want to alter the footprint of the porch to better suit your specific needs. Always check building and zoning restrictions if you are going to alter a house's footprint though; exceeding the original dimensions may get you in trouble if your house sits tight on its lot.

turn of the 20th century. Houses big enough to have servants often had a second set of stairs, which were usually narrow and very steep, that led to the kitchen directly from the servant's quarters, keeping the service staff's comings and goings separate from the family's. Today, these tiny stairways may be better used as storage spaces than redundant passageways from one floor to another.

Old-fashioned pantries and storage closets that once accomodated the way people shopped for and stored food are not always useful anymore. For example, a formal butler's pantry can be quite beautiful, but if you are really pressed for space or want a more functional kitchen/family room space, you may want to consider using the space for an informal dining area or family room. Small, inconvenient mudrooms that were located at the rear of many Bungalow kitchens as well as the back porches that some houses had are also excellent targets for potential reuse as part of a larger kitchen or a kitchen/family room area.

This well-designed kitchen renovation makes excellent use of what was once a closed-in porch, which included the window on the right. The newly created space now serves as a small mudroom and allows for an expanded family room area.

Using every bit of the wall space for storage became popular during the Victorian era and remained in style in Bungalows. A pantry space has an ingenious rolling library ladder for reaching the shelves. Located near the back door, the pantry makes for an ideal drop-off spot.

Mucking Around with Mudrooms

Most Bungalow-style houses have a formal entry at the front of the house and an informal entry at the rear. Just like in the old days when the iceman was expected to use the back door to drop off his delivery, we usually bring our household supplies in through the back of the house. Also, since cars are so much a part of our lives today, our garages are often located near the back of the house (if not actually attached to it), so most of us make our way from the car and garage to the house through the back door. This back door most often leads into the kitchen, and if you live in an old Bungalow-style house, you may also pass through an area that is often no larger than a coat closet: the mudroom.

Traditionally, a mudroom was a small, separate room, set between the back door of the house and the kitchen. In part, it served as an airlock, or buffer space, keeping the weather out of the house. It also helped keep other aspects of the outside world separate from the home, such as a farmer's muddy boots.

If you live in an old Bungalow-style house, you may feel that your little mudroom is a huge waste of space. It likely is cramped; it probably blocks light from your kitchen; and it doesn't provide enough space to conveniently store outdoor wear—or anything else—for that matter. In other words, it's a perfect space to usurp for some other purpose in your Bungalow kitchen. For example, by moving the back door over a few feet, you might create an efficient pantry closet, a tiny place for a desk, or enough room for a much bigger refrigerator.

On the other hand, mudrooms serve an important purpose. Yours may simply need updating, so you should consider how to make it a more efficient space, one that better suits your family's needs.

Putting the Food Away

Depending on the size of the house (and the size of the kitchen), the pantry in any given Bungalow can be a few designated shelves within the kitchen; a full closet used for storage for food, cookware, and other kitchen items; or its own room.

The butler's pantry, which is a separate room, has traditionally served as a staging area for serving meals between the kitchen and a formal

THE NEW MUDROOM

Although an old-fashioned mudroom may be the perfect space to gobble up for your new Bungalow kitchen, the fact is, a mudroom will develop by the back door whether you want it to or not. Kids will slough off their jackets and backpacks as soon as they come into the house, you'll drop the mail and the groceries as you rush to answer the telephone, and the family dog will know that this is the best place to beg for a walk. If you don't create a space to organize or cope with this kind of traffic, clutter, and dirt brought in from outside, it will accumulate somewhere else, probably in the kitchen, just as a Prairie farmer's mud might have collected there 100 years ago.

Today, modern mudrooms can be fairly large spaces that include a small powder room, a laundry area, or extra storage space. Conversely, a mudroom need not be a room at all; instead it can just be a small designated area within the kitchen but near the back door where coats can be hung, muddy shoes can be removed or snowy boots stored, and groceries can sit until they are put away.

In the mudroom that doubles as the entryway in this contemporary Bungalow, the stone tiles make a durable and attractive floor, while the beadboard walls and the stairway to the second floor contribute to a warm and welcoming entrance.

A roomy and useful pantry is located inside the back door of a casual lakeside Bungalow and around the corner from the kitchen, keeping much of the messier aspects of storage and cleanup out of the kitchen itself. The pass-through provides a friendly visual connection to the back door and those coming through it.

CUTE CHUTE

At first glance, this small door looks like a pet entry, but it's actually a laundry chute. In the layout of this kitchen renovation, the pantry was located directly over the laundry room in the basement. The owner discovered she loved this convenience for getting soiled dish towels and table linens to the laundry room without having to drag them down by hand. If you like this idea and your layout will accommodate it, make sure it's up to code (many local codes require that chutes be lined with metal in case of fire) and that it's large enough to handle tablecloths.

dining room. Often it is used for storing china and linen, and it provides counter space for serving out to the dining room. Sometimes pantries have a sink for additional cleanup, and some have even been retrofitted with a dishwasher and a small under-cabinet refrigerator for extra convenience. These rooms also serve as a buffer between the noise and clutter of the kitchen and the serenity of the dining room. If you entertain often, a butler's pantry can be a godsend.

Most people who live in early 20th-century Bungalows with original butler's pantries love the beauty and graciousness these spaces afford. If you have room in your layout and your lifestyle requires lots of room for cooking and serving, by all means, keep it. However, if what you really need is a bigger, more functional kitchen, a family room, a home office, or an informal dining room, then your old-fashioned butler's pantry may be the most logical space to use.

If storage is still a problem after you've decided what to do with your old (or possibly a new) pantry, an enormous number of possibilities exist for creating sufficient and beautiful pantry storage space just within the cabinetry itself, given the plethora of styles and formats available today. Or, a pantry closet can be built within the kitchen itself or in an area close by the kitchen such as an old mudroom, under a staircase, or in a small hallway.

Once-wasted space at the top of the basement stairs, which opens into the kitchen, has been turned into an efficient pantry. By taking advantage of the wall thickness, shallow shelving has been built into the cavity. When the door is closed, storage space is out of sight yet easily accessible.

Located just inside the rear entrance to the house, a mudroom features a playful peg rack and chalkboards, a perfect way to leave notes for family members as they're coming or going.

Revealing Structure

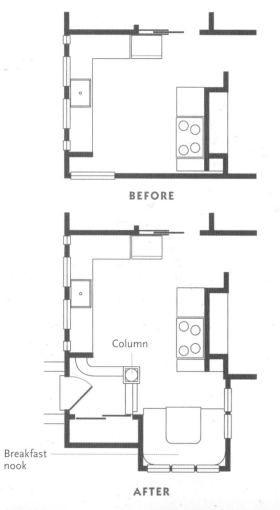

BEFORE

Column

Breakfast
nook

AFTER

Any time you break through an existing house wall, structural concerns need to be addressed, and generally speaking, if you knock a hole in an outside wall to connect a new space to it, you have to support the weight of what's above it with some kind of beam system. It's almost always possible to conceal the beam but at greater cost and with more complications.

This renovation and addition, in a Northern California Bungalow, could have been done without leaving the old house wall suspended from the ceiling (at right), but the architect and owners decided to reveal the remnant of the old house wall and support it with a hefty redwood column, a decision that also allowed them to make some choices that preserve the Arts and Crafts feeling of both the original house and the new kitchen. Redwood is a popular choice for wood trim in this part of the country, although it is usually used on the exterior, where its rot resistance is legendary. Here, redwood is used throughout the kitchen area as a trim material, so using it to clad the decorative supporting column was logical.

Although the architect chose to reveal original structure inside the house, on the outside he carefully matched the stucco siding material and the wood trim (at left), as well as the shape and massing of the addition, to the original house, so that no evidence exists that it was ever any different. There are different schools of thought about whether an addition should match the existing or be purposefully different, but I'll say it loud and proud: With Arts and Crafts-style architecture, make it look like it was always there!

The unusual built-in double pantry, part of an Arts and Crafts-style kitchen in a new house, flanks a functional office space that is both close to the kitchen yet discreetly hidden. Contemporary in design, the unique space is clearly Bungalow style in attitude, a perfect example of how to accommodate modern function yet maintain an old-fashioned aesthetic.

Adding On, Bungalow Style

When the space within the walls of your Bungalow won't let you do what you want and you've carefully considered every possible way to access space within your existing house but you still desperately want and/or need more room, then think about adding on. A few caveats: Building an addition to any house offers the greatest number of possibilities and solutions, but it usually requires the greatest budget. Also, an addition will take space away from your property and may require that you deal with zoning issues. Many cities and towns have building ordinances that limit what you can do in the way of an addition, so it's always best to check with your local building department before you get too lost in scheming.

Having said that, if you have the budget for an addition to create the kitchen you really want, your yard will withstand the loss of some space, and no legal issues block your plans, you can move on to the design of the addition. Even if you don't hire an architect, it's a good idea to consult with a design professional who specializes in antique houses. You want to add on to your home with sensitivity to your home's historical roots. Since most Bungalow kitchens are located in the rear, it makes sense that you'll be building either off the back of your Bungalow or on one side or the other toward the rear.

Still, in my opinion, if an addition doesn't improve the look of the whole house, it should be reconsidered and redesigned. Again, as with any aspect of working with old houses, the more you know about the appearance and structure of the original house, the more meaningful and appropriate the alterations will be.

The most common additions to Bungalows (and many other older houses) are informal dining areas and family rooms. The lynchpin to these additions is often a new kitchen, which most people want positioned between the new dining area or family room and the original formal dining room. With this arrangement, the kitchen can serve both areas easily. Also, keeping the kitchen within the original house allows the new exterior space, be it a family room or an informal dining room, to have the better light and views of the yard. Moreover, kitchens tend to need unbroken wall space for cabinetry, so keeping them within the confines of the existing footprint allows for use of the existing wall space.

A useful pantry is located in a mudroom closet just inside the back door of the house and steps from the kitchen. The sliding pocket door keeps the small, busy passage free.

The door to the pantry is fitted with textured art glass and made of richly hued wood that gives the space a unique Arts and Crafts look.

LESS IS MORE

Additions to houses can be any size, but sometimes a small bump-out can make an enormous difference, especially in a kitchen. Such a move may be so modest that it doesn't even require a full foundation, which makes it more affordable. Limited amounts of room gained in or near an existing kitchen, such as 2 ft. (the width of a conventional counter) along one wall, can translate into a great deal of storage space, a bank of windows, or a tiny dining nook.

A Bungalow/Tudor-style house features a three-story addition with a gable (located to the left of the front of the house) that is so well designed that it's hard to believe it wasn't always there. Although the addition extends only about 3 ft., it adds plenty of space for cabinets and windows in the new kitchen.

By adding on to the house instead of simply reusing existing space, you now have the ability to create a significantly larger kitchen, in addition to a new family room and/or an informal dining area. Also, with an addition, more options open up for how the whole house interacts with the yard, the garage, and wherever you park the car.

How to effectively combine and connect the garage, family room, dining room, and/or mudroom with a new kitchen is dependent on your budget, yard-to-house relationship, and the specific floor plan of your house. By becoming aware of the importance of the spaces that surround the kitchen, you can begin to explore how this all might work to best advantage in your Bungalow-style home.

Finding a Little Dining Room

Most original Bungalow-style houses have formal dining rooms, but many do not have informal eating spaces in the kitchen. Later Bungalows had breakfast nooks and banquettes; however, many other Bungalows— even large ones—did not have space in the kitchen for a table and chairs.

TIME GONE BY

At least once a week, the iceman delivered a block of ice, which was kept in an icebox either on the back porch or in the kitchen. In the summer, his horse pulled a wagon and in the winter, a sleigh.

Sometimes graceful solutions result from inspired renovations, like the small addition here that houses most of the kitchen's functional cabinetry. The decorative wooden arch that marks where the outsdide wall used to be is patterned on an original version that appears just inside the front door of this early Bungalow and hides the bearing beam.

The kitchen in this new Bungalow-style cabin in Maine opens into a friendly dining area, which, in turn, overlooks a lake. The owners wanted a modern-feeling interior, but they also sought an Arts and Crafts finish, which they achieved with the gentle arch and use of wood trim.

The functionality of the kitchen was enhanced exponentially by turning an old covered porch into a dining area, sunroom, and entryway that leads through French doors to parking and the backyard. A formal dining room is located at the opposite end of the kitchen, allowing the kitchen to serve both formal and informal eating spaces with ease.

Adding an informal dining area where one can drink a cup of coffee in the morning, serve kids a sandwich for lunch, or enjoy a light supper on a Sunday night is what most of my clients crave in their dream kitchens.

An informal dining area can be achieved in a number of ways by creatively rethinking spaces that already exist. Small kitchen islands, peninsulas, or built-in breakfast nooks can provide dedicated counter space for informal meals. Traditional Bungalow kitchens often featured freestanding furniture-style cabinetry, so the notion of placing a dining table within a Bungalow kitchen today is not only natural and appropriate but also a great way to showcase period furniture. Where space is at a premium, banquette-style seating used in conjunction with an informal dining table may be an ideal solution, as it was for many Bungalow kitchens in the 1930s.

If you need extra space to create your dining area, consider reclaiming an underused back porch, mudroom, or pantry. Finally, you may want to consider building a small bump-out, which in my experience is usually all that's necessary to house a perfect dining nook.

Family Rooms

Among my clients who are planning kitchen renovations, ironically, the one necessity they almost all require is a family room. The way we live in our kitchens today, most of us desire a space where family and friends can congregate that isn't right in the middle of the working kitchen. I have met only one client who desired her new kitchen to be isolated from her family, so she could cook in "peace." The rest of us like family rooms that work comfortably right next to the kitchen and that allow people to be near each other before and after meals.

Just as the notion of "the family room" is a new dimension to the Bungalow kitchen, so, too, is much of what furnishes a 21st-century family room. Today's family rooms often require television sets, CD players, computers, and all sorts of other electronic devices and media in order to work effectively for a contemporary family. These objects,

An informal dining area is tucked in the corner of a newly renovated kitchen in an early 20th-century Arts and Crafts house. The windows and French doors are in a small bump-out addition that provided the extra room necessary for the table and chairs. When the doors are open, diners feel as if they are eating outdoors.

A reclaimed porch provided the perfect location for this informal dining area, which is directly adjacent to the kitchen. Removing the table from the flow of the kitchen itself makes it a relaxing place for people to eat and still participate in kitchen activities. All the woodwork is made of new quartersawn cherry, which is in perfect keeping with the original 1913 Bungalow.

The owner of this lakeside Bungalow, once a 1920s cabin, wanted their kitchen to be connected to the dining area and the family room so that everyone could interact during meal preparation. Although the house is now virtually new, the owners underlined the original Bungalow style with paned windows, dark-stained rafters, and a plain (and essential) pillar that serves as a visual room divider.

BUNGALOW STYLE

EASY ACCESS

If we could, many of us would drive the car right into our kitchens to avoid lugging dry cleaning, sports equipment, and, of course, bags of groceries inside. Making a viable way to get from the car to the kitchen in the most comfortable and efficient way possible should be a top priority if you are building a kitchen addition.

One exercise I like to do with clients is have them visualize making their way inside from the car in the pouring rain with several bags of wet groceries and a clutch of crying children. This usually brings a vivid picture to mind, and the kitchen renovation project starts to become part of a much larger whole that often includes the kitchen, the back door, and a garage.

of course, would have seemed almost otherworldly to an original Bungalow's first inhabitants! At the same time, a family room in a new Bungalow needs to reflect the warmth and craftsmanship of an original Bungalow, including not only the characteristic Arts and Crafts detailing but also other homey items like a fireplace and cozy armchairs and sofas. Finally, bear in mind that a Bungalow family room does not need to be large, as long as it is comfortable.

Old Style, Modern Convenience

One final option is available to those of you who adore the Bungalow style, have a sufficient budget, and possess the time and the inclination, and that is to build your Bungalow-style dream house—and a Bungalow-style dream kitchen—from scratch. Starting fresh offers many benefits: a tight, dry foundation and basement; new electrical, heating, and plumbing systems; and the ability to avail yourself of the latest in energy-conserving building practices. Many sources of information on Bungalow design are available, and creating a new Bungalow that is every bit the peer of an original one is definitely possible.

The kitchen and family room in a renovated early 20th-century Bungalow once housed a tiny covered porch off a small, dark kitchen. Now, the rooms are separated by a half-wall. The dark wood floors, pillars, and trim allow the modern space to function comfortably with its original Bungalow past.

WHAT'S OLD IS NEW AGAIN

Today, several firms around the country are doing a logical thing: They are creating architectural plan sets for Bungalows just as Sears and other companies did 100 years ago and applying them to new Bungalow styles. The owners of these firms have spent time studying original Bungalows, so their design plans have the lines and critical feel of the originals. In fact, many of new Bungalows look very much like original early 20th-century houses, but they have been redesigned to meet modern expectations and standards, including larger bathrooms and kitchens, home offices, and master bedroom suites.

Just as many original Bungalows were built from designs purchased from architectural plan houses, these new plan sets provide a cost-effective alternative to hiring an architect.

A Craftsman Bungalow is ample proof that new construction can capture the essence of an old house. With the right design and the right builder, it's possible to start from scratch, add in all the elements you want, and have a brand-new house that rings true.

Of course, a brand-new Bungalow won't have the quirks, the "rock and roll," and the sense of history of an original. A new Bungalow kitchen may surpass the functions of an old one at every turn, but it will never have the vibe of an original. For some people this alone is a deal breaker, but for others, the idea of creating their own history is compelling. The decision is completely subjective.

Old-Fashioned Quality

For those who choose new construction, there are workmen today who build quality like they used to 100 years ago. It's possible to have a new Bungalow built that would rival the quality of the old ones. Manufacturers of high-quality Arts and Crafts building components can be found in various regions of the country, and architects, designers, and craftspeople who can build a new Bungalow on par with an original are eager to work.

As with many things, there are a few caveats: The cost of building something of the complexity of an original Bungalow is very high, and if you live in a part of the country where there isn't much old housing stock, then finding such skilled craftsmen may be a challenge. Still, working with an architect or designer (or on your own if you have the skill), you can create a new old Bungalow.

You can take advantage of all the technology and design information currently available to make a great space that still feels like it might always have been there. Not having to work around old wall locations and antiquated systems can make the process smoother and possibly quicker. You may lose some of the sense of history that an original Bungalow-style house will have, but you'll have the house of your dreams.

This beautiful Bungalow was originally a 1916 Sears kit house; specifically, the Ashmore model, one of the more elaborate houses in the Sears line. With enough resources, one could build a virtual duplicate of this house today, but it would lack the quality of age and history.

The owners played with old-fashioned elements such as pillars and dark woodwork to create the Arts and Crafts-style of the kitchen in a newly constructed house.

3 | FROM FLOOR TO CEILING: THE INTERIOR SHELL

Now that you've created a good working layout for your Bungalow kitchen, you need to take a close look at the area that will house the cabinetry, appliances, fixtures, and other design elements of your kitchen, specifically, the ceilings, walls, windows, doors, floors, and the trim that knit all these parts together. I call this area the "interior shell."

The materials you choose for the new Bungalow kitchen ceiling, walls, and floor must all work together and with the kitchen's appliances and layout to create the atmosphere you desire. Here, original Bungalow-style materials—subway tiles, linoleum, wood trim, leaded glass—combine to form a sleek, new Bungalow kitchen.

Depending on whether your kitchen opens directly onto another room or rooms dictates the choices you will make for these basic elements of the interior shell. Original Bungalow kitchens were specifically designed to be separated from the rest of the house. However, most Bungalow kitchens, even if the kitchen itself remains in the original footprint, are much more integrated with adjoining rooms, and the design choices for the kitchen reflect this intimacy. Therefore, keeping a harmonious blend of materials and colors for flooring, walls, trim, and even the ceiling will go a long way toward making your new kitchen look like it might always have been there.

The proper choices for materials for these basic elements should combine all the visual and tactile Arts and Crafts flavors evident in the rest of the Bungalow. Curiously, the essential materials for ceilings, walls, floors, and trim are pretty much the same (plaster, wood, tile, and glass), and it all depends on how you put them together.

But beware—much like the cooking that will take place in the Bungalow kitchen, too much of any one spice can overwhelm a dish, just as too much of one "art" or "craft" can defeat the practical elegance of a Bungalow kitchen.

Classic Ceiling Choices

If yours is an original early 20th-century Bungalow kitchen, it may well suffer from "lowered ceiling syndrome"—that is, at some point in its history the ceiling was dropped to cover up damage or new wiring or plumbing. If so, have no fear. Tearing down the old ceiling and reclaiming that lost real estate can be incredibly exciting. Bringing the room back to its original height not only opens up the room itself but also may open up your mind to all sorts of creative ideas to handle color, light, wall treatments, flooring, cabinetry, and lighting in the rest of the renovation. In any case, it's the perfect place to begin.

Even in an old Bungalow you can make the decision to vary from the original ceiling material if you are so inclined. Although most people like the idea of restoring the ceiling, it's not a law. With a new kitchen addition or when building a new home, you have a blank slate as far as the ceiling goes, and you should have fun with it.

Basic Plaster

Most original Bungalow kitchens had simple plaster ceilings. The plaster would have been troweled-over wood lath strips and finished smooth. Today, plaster ceilings are usually made of drywall with either a veneer

A view from the dining room into the kitchen of a San Francisco Bungalow reveals how a varied palette of materials conveys the handcrafted look of the Arts and Crafts style. Plaster walls, tile flooring, and stained cabinetry with art-glass glazing combine to bring the period to life.

Using raw materials in a Bungalow kitchen is the most direct way to convey the style. Here, a tin ceiling adds unexpected detail to an often overlooked element of a room's design.

coat of plaster or joint compound and tape. If your basic wall material choice is also plaster, you may decide to play with color or other design ideas.

In fact, with a basic plaster ceiling, you can entertain all sorts of decorative possibilities. Rough-coat plaster, which has a visible texture, was popular in original Bungalow kitchens and is a good choice for the Bungalow style. Creating a recessed tray is another way to add visual interest. Adding shallow beams that are either painted or stained with a natural finish on the ceiling can also add an Arts and Crafts touch.

Tin

Although tin was not frequently used in the earliest Bungalow kitchens, today tin (and synthetics made to look like tin) ceilings are popular in Bungalow-style houses, adding a period feeling. The busy-ness of the texture of the tin panels can be somewhat distracting if the rest of the kitchen finishes are simple. At the same time, when your ceiling is the most interesting element in your kitchen, it creates an unexpected design choice. Any balance issues can be resolved with more neutral color choices.

Tin ceilings can pose a few problems. Sound tends to bounce easily off tin, and thus a tin ceiling can add more noise to the natural din of a kitchen. And remember that tin panels must be laid out in a rather rigid grid. If your ceiling is not smooth or perfectly aligned, the tin panels

Taking it from the top

If you are renovating an existing Bungalow kitchen, chances are the original ceiling is hiding above the one you can presently see. In many Bungalow kitchens, as the original ceiling began to deteriorate, owners found it easier (and less expensive) to simply cover up the original. The "new" ceiling may have been simply another layer of plaster or perforated cardboard tiles nailed on to wooden strapping and, in turn, nailed directly over the original ceiling.

However, especially if the kitchen required new plumbing or wiring, a dropped ceiling, created with acoustic paneling, was often devised to hide the new fixtures. This sort of ceiling was relatively easy to install and hid a multitude of sins. Also, a lower ceiling made it easier to replace cabinetry. The new cabinets could be installed flush with the new ceiling, eliminating the dreaded "dust shelf" and without creating the need for a soffit.

The tops of the cabinets meet the edge of the tray ceiling, which appears taller because of the coffer. This gives the whole bank of cabinets a seamless, built-in appearance, typical of later Bungalow kitchens and perfect in a new one.

may not lay down properly. Also, extra care has to be exercised in laying out ceiling lighting. Whether you are using recessed lights, pendants, or surface-mounted fixtures, the locations of the fixtures need to be figured out carefully in the rough-wiring stage so the finished fixtures relate properly to the installed panels. The smaller the grid, the more careful you have to be to get the fixtures in the right place. This usually requires drawing out the grid on the rough ceiling so the electrical boxes can be accurately located.

Most tin ceilings are designed with companion crown moldings that soften the transition from the ceiling to the walls, and, when done properly, the effect can be quite beautiful. Bear in mind that it's tough to use tin tiles in conjunction with plaster or wood ceiling elements. The tin tiles are meant to be their own complete system.

Wood

Wood is a rather unusual material choice for a ceiling, but when used creatively it can be a particularly beautiful choice, as well as historically evocative even though it was not actually used on the ceilings of original Bungalow kitchens.

Wood plank and wooden beadboard are both viable variations that are right in keeping with the Bungalow style. A wood plank ceiling

Horizontal planking lines the walls and ceiling in this lakeside cabin. Painted creamy yellow, the rustic walls underscore the casual beauty of this vacation-style Bungalow kitchen.

PLASTER, TIN, OR WOODEN BEAMS

Because most original Bungalow kitchen ceilings were *plaster*, chances are good that yours was, too. However, depending on the age of your Bungalow, at some point it may have been lined with pressed tin panels.

If you find old *tin panels* on your ceiling and they are in reasonably good shape, you might even be able to save the entire ceiling. If not, reproduction tin panels are readily available and easy to install.

A Bungalow hallmark, *ceiling beam systems* can be an interesting way to dress up an otherwise blank kitchen ceiling. Many of these beam styles were available from millwork catalogs in the early 20th century as stock pieces and could be assembled by a carpenter on site with relative ease. Whole trim systems can be purchased for entire rooms.

Parts of the beam systems are just flat stock, and the rest are made up of machined moldings, reasonable facsimiles of which are still available from a number of millwork companies, lumberyards, and home centers. Use old catalogs, available as reprints, as guides to creating new versions of the old patterns.

The type of beadboard on this Bungalow ceiling was often used in carriage houses, barns, storage areas, and porch ceilings, so it is associated with more informal, practical settings. The original ceiling here was plaster, but the beadboard treatment is new. The rich, warm natural wood has an antique elegance that adds to the ambience of the kitchen.

contributes nicely in a more rustic Bungalow kitchen, especially if the walls are covered with the same material.

Beadboard was a traditional material for covering porch ceilings in the late 19th and early 20th centuries, as well as for use as walls and ceilings in carriage houses, attics, and work structures. It works easily in the equally practical kitchen environment Wood is the kind of natural material that the Arts and Crafts movement advocated, and whether it is painted or finished with a stain, it can work comfortably with a wide variety of wall, floor, trim, and cabinet choices.

Other Ceiling Materials

Original Bungalow kitchen ceilings were occasionally finished (or refinished) in myriad materials, including cork panels, tile, and wallpaper-on-plaster. Used judiciously and creatively, these materials also work well on a Bungalow kitchen ceiling. It's important to bear in mind, though, that the busier a ceiling is, the more it tends to bear down on those who view it, which creates an uncomfortable sensation. Even with a high ceiling, if it is overly decorated, it will compete with many other important kitchen elements, including cabinetry, lighting, and appliances, so it's a good idea to balance your choices.

BUNGALOW STYLE

DOUBLE DUTY

The ceiling in this new Bungalow kitchen is working double time. At first glance, it appears to be lovely but simple beamed. But on close inspection, it's clear that it presents an interesting solution for creating a higher ceiling in an otherwise short space. These ceiling beams are not just ornamental; they are the joists for the floor above, and the wooden ceiling itself is the underside of the finished second floor. Had this ceiling been done conventionally, valuable space would have been lost in adding wood strapping and a finished plaster surface.

Because the ceiling is "open," the electrical wiring was left exposed. These owners adopted the attitude, "If you can't hide it, flaunt it". They chose a contemporary style of lighting. And the notion of honesty with materials is very much in keeping with the Bungalow ethic, and, in this case, the modern solution meshes well with the older look.

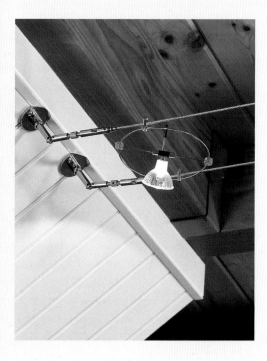

The smooth plaster walls have been painted a rich cream color, while the plaster ceiling has been painted white, creating the illusion of height. The neutral walls together with the white trim around the windows and door openings set off the warm cherry cabinetry, much the way white walls set off art being displayed in a gallery.

The Walls Around You

It's impossible to choose materials for walls in a Bungalow kitchen without having already considered the ceiling because the two are so closely related. But this doesn't mean that the ceiling and walls must be the same material. The two elements just have to work well together.

Plaster

Plaster—real plaster or drywall that has a skim coat of plaster—is a fine choice for a wall material, especially in smaller kitchens. The look of plaster can be simulated to some extent with drywall panels that are sealed with joint compound and tape, but nothing beats the smooth, seamless look of a good plaster job. Particularly if you are investing a great deal of time, effort, and money in your new kitchen, don't skimp on the quality of the plaster; your penny-wise choice will come back to haunt you.

Plaster is a relatively forgiving and easily repairable material. If you don't plan your wiring or plumbing accurately in the rough stage of construction or if you want to add a light fixture or some other element after your renovation is finished, you can open up plaster walls and repair them without much difficulty. Whether your plaster finish is smooth or rough, it will be flat enough to make the application of wood trim easy. Any resulting gaps between plaster and wood can be seamlessly caulked and painted.

The surface of a plaster wall can be treated in many different ways, too. Most obviously, it can be painted, either directly on top, or it can be tinted when it's mixed so that the color goes all the way through the material, a technique that was popular in the days of original Bungalow construction that gives depth to the color.

The surface of the plaster may be smoothed (although a mirror-smooth surface can appear too "slick" for a Bungalow-style kitchen) or left textured so that the strokes of the plasterer's blade remain.

Wood

For Bungalow kitchen walls, wood makes an appropriate material, especially in larger spaces that include a family room or dining area because, like any wall material, it can be used to visually connect the entire area Wood is often combined with plaster or tile to create a classic Arts and Crafts look.

Wainscot why and how

Wainscot is a wood wall covering, often designed as part of a chair rail (about 3 ft. from the floor), but sometimes as part of a plate rail (several feet from the ceiling). The area between the chair rail or plate rail and the floor is known as the dado, which is infilled with wainscot. Beadboard, either painted or stained naturally, has long been a classic material for wainscoting.

Wainscoting was a popular decorative device in Colonial and Victorian houses, including the kitchens, but for sanitary reasons, wainscoting was kept out of early Bungalow kitchens. Nevertheless, wainscoting was an extremely popular wall covering throughout the rest of the house, and as a result, it is an excellent decorative choice in a contemporary Bungalow kitchen, especially as a way to integrate a family room, dining room, or other adjacent area.

White wainscot in the dining room matches the trim in the kitchen, its "board" pattern the relative width of the door casing, so that the eye makes a visual connection between the adjacent rooms.

Wood can serve as a wainscot, or it can be used to panel the entire wall. Wood wainscot is applied in a horizontal band or "dado" of wood below the chair rail molding—usually as high as the back of a chair. Beadboard was a popular choice for wainscoting, and today it remains an attractive, affordable choice.

Painted plank walls, like plank ceilings, can work well in more rustic settings. Left natural, they are a little too informal. Also, rooms that are entirely made of natural finished wood can feel heavy or boxlike. Nevertheless, when done with a balance of light (natural or otherwise) and softer elements (like wallpaper or a pale plaster wall nearby), the effect can be nicely dramatic.

Beadboard was a common material in kitchens of the late Victorian period and often showed up in early Bungalow houses. Here, the painted beadboard walls give the open shelving a sense of elegance yet make the space feel more intimate and informal.

Handcrafted tile in the Arts and Craft style add a warm, textured touch that provides a pleasant contrast to the high-tech stainless appliances in this 1930s-era California Bungalow kitchen.

Horizontal planking lines the walls in this lakeside cabin. Painted a creamy yellow, the rustic walls underscore the casual beauty of this vacation-style Bungalow kitchen.

In original Bungalows, these wood elements were common throughout the rest of the house; indeed many of them were characteristic of Bungalows. Although such work did not often show up in original Bungalow kitchens, the kitchen is the perfect place for it.

Tile

Tile is an excellent choice for a Bungalow kitchen wall material, whether it is used for practical purposes or decorative ones. Covering the walls of an entire kitchen with it can result in a cold, antiseptic feeling, so this is less often done. But combining tile and plaster can result in a pleasing balance since the two materials work well together. The smooth, open look of plaster helps the room to relax visually and allows the tile to function as an accent in selected areas.

The most obvious place where tile comes into play is at the backsplash, where the tile seals the gap between the back of the countertop and the wall, and protects wet and hot areas in the kitchen. Here the identifying colors, textures, and patterns of the Arts and Crafts style can be shown to best effect. It's important to remember, though, that Arts and Crafts tile can be quite costly, so you may choose to use it sparingly or place it where it will not be damaged from water or heat.

Tile can also be used for selected wall surfaces beyond the confines of the backsplash. One area in the kitchen where wall tile has long been a logical and practical choice is around freestanding stoves and ranges. This kind of hardworking decorative touch is a hallmark of the Bungalow style.

Floors

When we enter a room, the floor is often the first thing we see. It's the anchor for the room, both visually and functionally, and in some ways it is a darker mirror of the ceiling, so the material you choose for your flooring is essential to the whole design of the room.

As with ceilings and walls, wood and tile were common materials for floors in original houses, as was linoleum, which was newly popular in the United States. Taking cues from the past, tile, wood, and linoleum

White crackle-glazed antique wall tiles are a practical and timeless addition to any Bungalow-style kitchen.

Handmade tiles add not only texture but also color to a Bungalow-style kitchen. Here, matte tiles in natural tones that are intrinsic to the style soften the dark hue and the highly reflective polished marble countertop.

remain obvious choices for Bungalow kitchen floors and stand up well to the rigors of kitchen traffic, while conveying the characteristics of the Bungalow style.

Wood

Even if you plan to use a lot of wood in your kitchen, the floor offers the perfect location for more of this characteristic Bungalow material. Strip wood flooring has been a classic since the mass manufacture of house materials in the mid-19th century. Oak is the default choice that has long been a standby, and for good reason: It's hard, stands up well to use and abuse, takes stain well, and feels good on stocking feet.

Nothing screams "contemporary" like bright oak flooring with a high-gloss finish—the classic condominium look. This approach is best avoided in a Bungalow kitchen. Oak looks better with a medium brown stain that brings out the beauty of the wood grain and fits into the natural tones of the Bungalow color palette. If the color of the floor is even just slightly darker than the cabinetry and the rest of the wood trim in the kitchen, it will offer a meaningful contrast and provide a darker base that will anchor the look of the room.

Original Bungalow floors were often stained wood finished with paste wax for protection against abrasion. Since wax needs to be frequently reapplied and polished, most people today opt for matte-finish polyurethane. This finish lasts quite a long time and comes closer to the look of wax than any other. A simple trick is to apply the first two of three coats of urethane in gloss finish, and then use matte finish for the top coat. The gloss finish is harder than the matte and forms a solid and long-lasting base.

Fir is also an appropriate flooring choice for a Bungalow kitchen and was often a stock choice for original Bungalows. The long running grain pattern of fir looks particularly good in painted kitchens since there is no other wood grain to compete with. Fir is softer than oak and was in its day a lower-cost alternative that was sometimes used as a subfloor for linoleum or for painted floor cloths. With reasonable care, it provides a solid and beautiful finished floor in today's kitchen.

Wood floors bring warmth and richness to any room. And since most dining and family room floors feature hardwood, using it in the kitchen is a smart way to tie the spaces together.

The long-running grain of fir planking combines handsomely with quartersawn cherry used in the cabinetry of a 1913 Bungalow kitchen.

TIME GONE BY

Painted floor cloths, often made of oilcloth, were popular at the turn of the 19th century and served as a colorful and easy way to dress up any kitchen floor. They could be washed much more easily than a wool or cotton carpet. This also satisfied the "sanitary bug" that was so prevalent at the time.

Rugs manufactured by the Congoleum Company® were a cross between sheet linoleum and old-fashioned oilcloth floor coverings. Like linoleum, these water-resistant and easy-to-clean floor coverings were available in a variety of patterns and colors and were a popular and economical choice in original Bungalow kitchens.

Found Flooring

When this 1919 Bungalow kitchen was renovated, its original floor plan was altered considerably, incorporating the space that had once been a large pantry into the rest of the kitchen. This was accomplished by removing an important central wall.

When a new wall is constructed, the "sole plate" (or bottom) of the wall is nailed directly onto the subfloor and then the finished floor is laid down on top. If the wall is later removed, as this one was, a scar will be left where the wall once stood, and that sole plate hole must be patched in order for the new floor to be smooth. This isn't a big problem in a newer house where flooring material can be easily matched. However, in an older house, finding antique flooring of a similar age, grain, and type can be challenging. Fortunately, in many original Bungalow houses, no more than two or three varieties of wood flooring were used throughout the house, and similar flooring can frequently be found in some other room.

In this case, the owner located wood in his attic floor that was identical to that in his kitchen. If you are faced with having to locate some patching for a scarred old floor, try looking in the attic, in upstairs hallways, inside closets, or in other out-of-the way areas to see if you can "steal" a few pieces. Patch the area where you "stole" the planks with wood of the same thickness, and then use your salvage where it really matters.

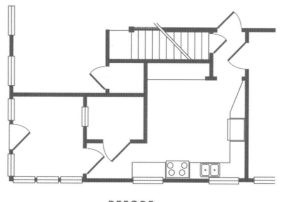

BEFORE

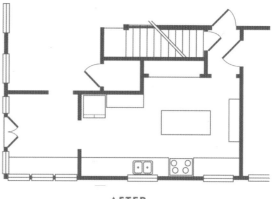

AFTER

Congoleum floor covering rugs were a colorful, affordable, and durable alternative to wool rugs.

Linoleum

Linoleum was fairly new during the prewar Bungalow period and remains a smart flooring choice for a kitchen. Unlike the sheets of vinyl that became a low-cost flooring option in the 1950s, linoleum is a natural, nonallergenic material that is made of jute fibers and linseed oil and fits well within the Bungalow aesthetic. In recent years, in large part due to its green properties, high-quality linoleum has enjoyed renewed popularity. Also, the craft of designing floors with linoleum, including inlaying various colors and painting on the linoleum, is now much esteemed and is one of the most exciting facets of the Bungalow kitchen.

Patterned linoleum was generally the style that would have been found in an original Bungalow, but solid colors also work well. Linoleum is soft underfoot, resilient (glassware and china won't easily break if dropped), easy to clean, and can provide an opportunity to bring the earth tones so integral to the Bungalow style into your kitchen. There are lots of

As a flooring material, linoleum can add a new dimension of color to the kitchen. Here, the red accent squares offset the traditional elements like beadboard and white trimwork.

Black linoleum flecked with gray provides a bold stroke on the floor of a renovated pre-1920s Bungalow kitchen. This is sheet linoleum, meaning that it was purchased in large rolls and then glued to the floor.

Tile floors were popular in original Bungalows located in California. In a renovated Bungalow kitchen in San Francisco, the slate tile and Craftsman-style cabinetry create a pleasing rusticity among the modern appliances.

TIME GONE BY

Linoleum was invented in Staines, England, in 1860 by Frederick Walton, who formed the Linoleum Manufacturing Company in 1864. Due to its durability, water resistance, and relatively low cost, linoleum enjoyed instant popularity. Made of solidified linseed oil (linoxyn) combined with cork or wood flour and applied over a burlap or canvas backing, linoleum became a practical flooring material in high-use areas, especially in kitchens, and was perhaps the most common flooring material in original Bungalow kitchens.

Linoleum is very malleable and can be cut and combined with complementary colors and patterns in an infinite variety of designs, styles, and colors. The border pattern on this floor is a classic design, meant to imitate wool rugs used in more formal rooms in the house, and is a style frequently used in original Bungalow kitchens.

ways to work with linoleum by combining different colors, patterns, and even by painting it. Vinyl flooring can simulate the look of linoleum depending on the pattern, but nothing beats the authentic look and feel of real linoleum in a Bungalow kitchen.

Tile was a choice that was highly recommended for the kitchen floor during the Bungalow's early years. It fit all the criteria for the style, being affordable, a "natural" material, and a great vehicle for patterns and colors that were popular at the time. Mission-style Bungalows, located predominantly in the Southwest, were the first to feature tile as a flooring option for any style house. In the Northeast, a tile floor can be cool on bare feet in the summertime. Laid over a radiant-heating system, warm tile is a cozy extra in the winter months.

MAKING AN ENTRANCE

Because Bungalows were built in such quantities, there is a strong market for antique period doors. At the same time, new doors in original Bungalow styles are available in most local home centers and lumberyards at reasonable prices. As a result, the choices are all yours. If you find a stunning antique door, you may want to incorporate it into a new Bungalow kitchen, but be mindful of its relationship to the other doors in your house. Equally, if you are renovating an original Bungalow kitchen but need a new door, you very likely can find an appropriate one easily and economically.

Doors

Doors are another of the identifying elements of a Bungalow kitchen that can add a great deal to the overall look of your project. The patterns that were popular at the time of the original Bungalows have simple characteristics that speak to the straightforward aesthetic of the Arts and Crafts movement. The most common type of interior door in Bungalow-style homes has five evenly spaced horizontal raised panels inset into simple stiles and rails. Bungalow kitchen doors used as passage from room to room are typically 6 ft. 8 in. high by 2 ft. 6 in. wide, whereas doors to pantries or closets are often narrower.

Within the Bungalow kitchen style, kitchen doors are frequently removed from the doorways that lead to the adjacent rooms, leaving just the doorways themselves to mark the transitions. The reason is that today we congregate in the kitchen, so its direct connection to adjacent rooms is important. Doors stem flow, and while they were an important and key design element in the past, today they simply get in the way. Regardless of whether you choose to keep doors in their original doorway openings, you'll most likely need to think about doors for storage spaces, pantries, the mudroom, the basement, or leading to the backyard.

A five-panel pantry door, a classic Bungalow element, is outfitted with period hardware to complete the look.

Interior doors were available in a number of patterns for original Bungalows. Some of these patterns are still available from building-supply catalogs and from lumberyards and home centers. Interior doors are almost always 1⅜ in. thick and typically 2 ft. 6 in. wide by 6 ft. 8 in. tall. Given this convention, it is fairly easy to find an old or a new door to fit your doorway.

Practical Design Considerations

A few factors should be considered when choosing doors for your kitchen. Style is certainly one, and if you are renovating an original Bungalow kitchen, then you'll probably want to use a pattern that fits the style of the rest of your house. If you had a doorway into your kitchen that you'd like to have fitted with a door (whether there was one originally there or not), then it will most likely be seen next to other doors, and you'll want it to match or at least make it blend well. If you can't find a new replacement that matches, then you might want to explore salvage yards and other places that deal with historic woodwork.

Doing a search of these salvage or "architectural antique" stores can yield all kinds of treasures in addition to finding the doors you are after. Hardware, woodwork, lighting, windows, you name it, many of these original pieces can often be found for reasonable amounts of money. If you can't find an original door for your kitchen that matches the rest of your doors, the last resort is to have one custom made. Custom millwork shops exist everywhere, and although the door you need won't be cheap, sometimes it's worth it to have one that matches the rest of your Bungalow. Getting these details right makes a big difference in the final result of a renovation project.

The handsome oak door leads from the newly renovated kitchen to the back porch of a 1916 Midwestern Bungalow. Although the door is new, its design—the six-paned window over paneled wood—is a classic Bungalow style and provides the perfect balance of light with solidity.

A standard Bungalow exterior door is crafted from white pine and has simple beveled glass lights. The panels are also plain, in keeping with the style.

Wood species is another consideration in door choice. The door patterns that you see in old catalogs (and new ones) were (and are) available in a number of wood species. Oak was an extremely popular choice for Bungalows, but poplar, pine, and fir were also seen quite often. If your kitchen is done in a natural finished wood, then matching not only the door's style but also its wood type is important, too.

The Back Door

You'll need to plan for at least one exterior door if your Bungalow kitchen has direct access to the outdoors either through the kitchen or an adjacent space like a mudroom or family room. Exterior doors are typically wider and more substantial than interior doors with a standard of 2 ft. 8 in. to 3 ft. wide as the norm. Exterior doors are also thicker than interior doors at 1¾ in.

Many of the beautiful exterior doors on original Bungalows have been replaced over the years with inferior versions that beg to be upgraded. Most building codes will allow you to replace a narrower exterior door with one of the same size in a renovation or restoration project, but work in an addition or in totally new construction will almost always require a door that is three feet wide for fire safety purposes.

Windows

Windows are a major design element when it comes to defining the Bungalow kitchen. Even if your walls, ceiling, and flooring are not authentically Bungalow style, your kitchen can still be complete with the right windows.

The basic window styles found in original Bungalows are double hung, casement, and fixed-light windows. Many of the "pure" Bungalows, particularly the pre-World War I houses, have smaller windows that contribute to the cozy feel of the style. These smaller windows allowed for more wall space and woodwork on the interior, which accounted for the snug feeling of these homes. The downside is that this effect comes at the expense of natural light and can often make the house feel dark.

On the other hand, Bungalows often had larger windows in the kitchen. Architects and builders of the time realized that kitchens needed more light for basic visibility as well as for a sense of "cheerfulness" that was in contrast with the other more formal rooms in the house. The sink area has long been established as the one place where the homemaker spent most of her time in the kitchen. Between preparing food and cleaning

Using a pair of double-hung six-over-one windows is an ideal way to create a larger window opening while staying true to the Bungalow style. The divided light upper sash over the single sheet of glass in the lower sash remains in the Bungalow vocabulary.

up after meals, the sink gets a lot of use. Consequently, groupings of windows above the sink provided refreshing views of the outdoors and allowed in necessary daylight for kitchen tasks.

Double-Hung Windows

Double-hung windows derive their name from the fact that they are comprised of two vertically hung sashes held in a frame. The window jambs provide the track pieces that support the sash frames, which in turn support the glazing, or window glass. The wooden pieces that divide the individual pieces of glass are called muntins.

The number of "lights" or pieces of glass that are in each sash frame identifies double-hung windows. A "six over one" double-hung window means that there are six pieces of glass in the upper sash and one in the lower. Many Bungalows had multiple lights in the upper sash and just one below. Some of these windows have playful upper-sash arrangements that go beyond the standard symmetrical ones that you might expect.

Originally, double-hung windows were "single glazed" with just one layer of glass in the frame. Insulation for cold months came from storm windows. While this is still a good system, today, more options that hold true to old windows are available. Double-glazed or "thermo pane" windows have a sandwich of two pieces of glass with a vacuum-sealed cavity between them. "True divided lights" have individual sandwiches of sealed glass in each of the openings created by the muntins. These can look great but are costly, and those sealed sandwiches will eventually fail and the panes will fog.

Three over the Sink

It's rare to see large expanses of glass in Bungalow kitchens that look right, but there are always exceptions. In the past, the way of getting more light into the kitchen was by pairing up or creating groupings of conventionally sized windows. Three windows became the norm and the classic style. Particularly over a sink, these kinds of groupings provide views of the outdoors and bring some visual relief into the kitchen.

While it's typical to see sets of three windows over a sink, any number that your wall will accommodate will work. However, wall space is

All kitchens struggle to balance the need for wall space for cabinetry and storage with the desire for natural light. The area above the kitchen sink often wins, and, in Bungalows, a bank of three windows was a common—and now a classic—choice.

BUNGALOW BASICS

Muntins

Muntins are strips of wood separating panes of glass in a sash. In early Bungalow design, a divided light sash was an important concept. Although it was certainly possible for manufacturers to make glass in large sheets in the early 20th century, the Arts and Crafts style dictated that windows reflect their craftsmanship. Muntins (as well as colored glass) in windows offered an opportunity to use pattern and design in creative configurations. Variations on the Bungalow-style divided-light theme are infinite, and old window and millwork catalogs can provide scores of ideas.

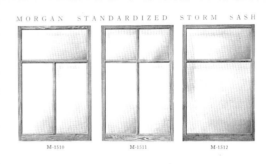

MORGAN STANDARDIZED STORM SASH

M-1510   M-1511   M-1512

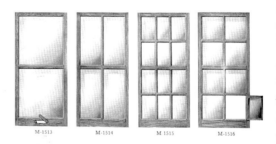

M-1513   M-1514   M-1515   M-1516

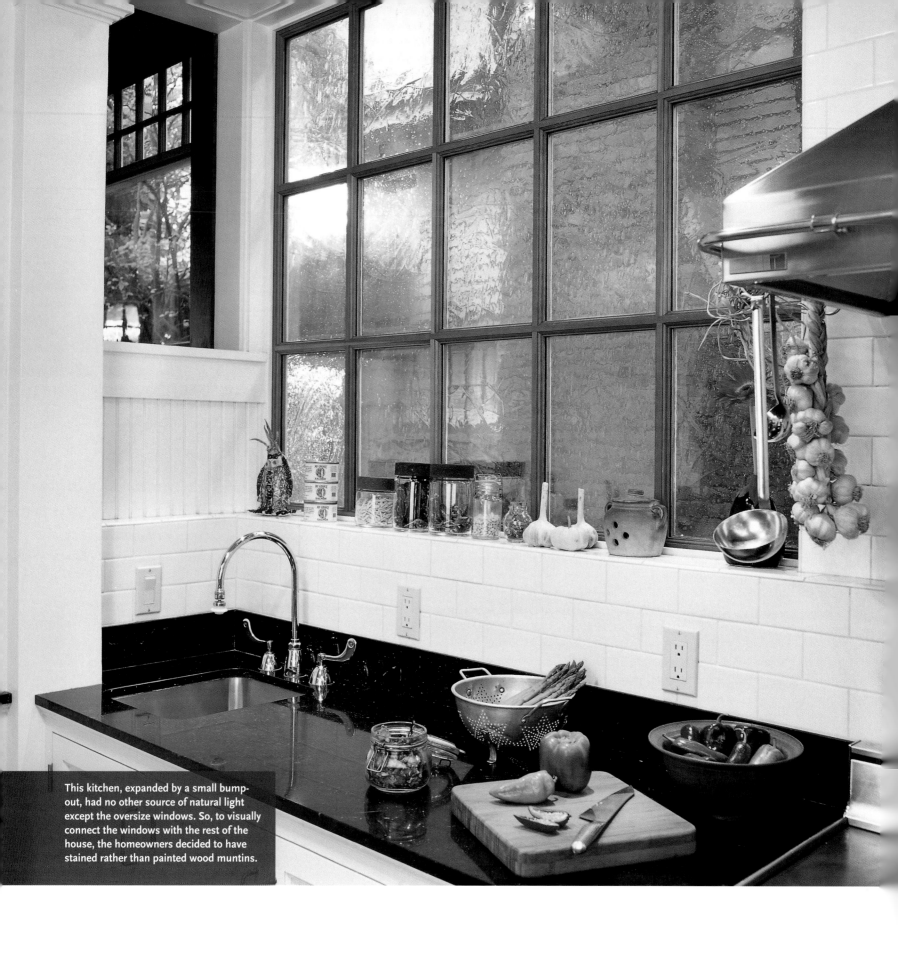

This kitchen, expanded by a small bump-out, had no other source of natural light except the oversize windows. So, to visually connect the windows with the rest of the house, the homeowners decided to have stained rather than painted wood muntins.

always at a premium in a Bungalow kitchen, where the desire for natural light and views competes with the need for wall storage. If your kitchen layout will allow, wrap windows around the corner of the room by the sink for a dramatic effect and twist on a conventional look.

Casement Windows

A close companion of the double-hung window in a Bungalow kitchen is the casement window. Casements swing on hinges that allow the entire window to open, where with a double-hung window, only one sash can be fully open at a time. Most casements are built to open out, although some of the old ones are hinged to open in.

The traditional Bungalow-style set of three windows over the sink is given a fresh twist. Two narrow one-over-one double-hung windows flank a larger fixed sash with an Arts and Crafts-inspired muntin design. A fourth double-hung window wraps around the corner, allowing in even more light and expanding the views.

Finding hardware for casement windows can be an added adventure. If they are the type that swing out, they'll likely require stays to keep them in place. There are a number of companies that make reproduction casement hardware. It's worth the extra effort to maintain or rejuvenate old casements because they are especially nice for catching cool breezes in the summer months.

Both casement and double-hung windows can be arranged in interesting combinations that work well with the Bungalow vocabulary. To get more light into the kitchen and still stay true to the style, combining duplicate pairs of windows does the trick nicely. Combinations of three or more can also work well, as can a triptych composition, where the window in the middle is more prominently designed than its flanking members. This is a tried-and-true device in the Arts and Crafts tradition.

The casement conundrum

One of the issues with old-style casement windows is deciding how to deal with window screens. Unless you rarely open the windows, you will need screens. New casement windows have sophisticated crank mechanisms that operate underneath the actual moving window sash, so the screen can be fixed on the inside of the window, assuming that the window will open out. The out-swing window is usually preferable, since the open window does not intrude on your interior space. However, old casement windows are another issue. The crank mechanisms on these antique windows are often just adjustable metal slides that keep the window from being blown shut. One screen solution that is simple and effective: Hinge the screen like a small door so it can open in to allow access to the slide hardware.

In this 1920s Bungalow kitchen, a classic set of three windows—all original—over the kitchen sink is handled "casement style." The two outside sashes are operable, while the middle one is fixed. These charming old windows, like many old casements, lack crank mechanisms and open like small doors.

Here is a luxurious variation on the classic Bungalow-style three-windows-over-the-sink: three operable pairs of casement windows along an entire wall. A fourth single window wraps the corner to the left. The three period-style wall sconces over the six-paned casement windows balance the theme and result in a dramatic flood of light.

This dramatic arrangement looks antique but is actually a new set of windows in a renovated original Bungalow. In another variation on the three-windows-over-the-sink idea (with a fourth window wrapping the corner), the flanking sashes are casement windows, but the large middle window is fixed. The casement windows, with four parallel muntins above a clear pane, open out and screens are on the inside. The screens are hinged like small doors and need to be opened to allow access to the windows themselves, a slightly cumbersome but charming setup.

OLD CATALOGS, NEW STYLE

If a trip to the local salvage yard doesn't net any satisfying discoveries, you may have to custom fabricate select pieces. Stained glass is one example. If you need to have a specific size window piece for your project, finding proper patterns can be tricky. Unless you are lucky enough to find a knowledgeable stained-glass artist who would have authentic Bungalow-era patterns at hand, you may have to lead the way.

Reprints of old building-material catalogs are readily available and can provide a number of patterns that are appropriate. These designs can be copied exactly, or they can be used as a reference for having your own interpretation made. Stained glass is just one of the many materials that are represented in old catalogs; you'll also find many examples of doors, windows, flooring, trim, and molding profiles in these books. They are a great investment.

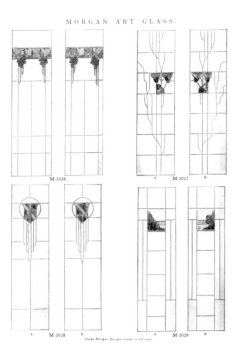

Although the window is original to this 1917 Bungalow, the stained glass is new. The upper sash has an unusual muntin arrangement of four tall glass bays, which were used for a Frank Lloyd Wright-inspired stained-glass pattern.

Located in a dining room adjacent to the kitchen, a 10-light, fixed-sash window is original to this renovated 1920s Bungalow. Windows such as this one serve double duty, both as a source of light and as a decorative object in a room, which is why they often have stained glass. Horizontal fixed-sash windows are generally located higher up in a wall to allow for furniture below, such as a sideboard, or for privacy.

Stained Glass

Stained and leaded glass has its place in Bungalow kitchen windows, too. There are a number of motifs unique to the Bungalow style that were commercially available when Bungalow popularity was at its height. Typically, these decorative glass pieces were in fixed light sashes and located where privacy, not views, was desirable. Or they were placed higher up in the wall to work as a source of light while providing wall space for furniture. With its lack of ostentation, stained glass holds a strong place in the Arts and Crafts tradition, representing the honest hand-wrought art that was rendered so beautifully by humble craftsmen.

Trim

Trim is the woodwork that includes door and window casings, baseboard, ceiling moldings and beams, chair rails, and other decorative moldings, as well as applied flat trim on the walls that complete the kitchen's appearance. It's really the last step in the process of finishing off the look of the kitchen. (Cabinetry must also be considered in the trim design, which will be discussed in chapter 4.)

White wood trim and wainscot in the breakfast nook of this new Bungalow create a pleasing contrast with the rich hues of the stained flooring and table. The trim in a new Bungalow is done in a characteristic style, where each of the door openings as well as the windows are bordered by flat wood trim, then painted white.

Here's a real study in wood species and how the Bungalow style of trim creates a beautiful and unifying system. Look carefully at the wood column to the right (see the photo above), its capital, and the horizontal boxed beam above. These flat stock wood trim pieces are made of quartersawn oak and are stained a golden brown. The oak trim is the same style that is used throughout this new Bungalow-style house (see the photo on the facing page). The cabinetry and related woodwork in the kitchen are done in cherry. The two species of wood nestle against each other. The trim carries the theme established in the house all the way around the kitchen. The flat stock of the trim mirrors the paneling style of the kitchen woodwork.

"Flat stock" casing, or casing that has no profile to it, was the preferred style of trim in Bungalow houses and so in their kitchens. This almost Shaker style of simplicity was a key component in the look of the trim system that was an integral part of the concept of honest materials expressing themselves in a straightforward fashion. Using patterns and layers of flat casings can be very beautiful and is instantly identified with the Bungalow style.

The trim systems in Bungalow kitchens are yet another device to really nail the style and bring a stamp of authenticity to a Bungalow kitchen. So it is necessary to look to the Bungalow's formal rooms to provide examples of what might be appropriate. Here is an opportunity for some creativity in the way that you interpret your new kitchen space.

Think about trim in your Bungalow kitchen in one of two ways. The first is to use the basic outlines of doors, windows, and other spaces as a guide. The best wood used to trim around these openings is almost always flat stock that can be either painted or finished naturally. The flat stock casing is used as a border around the windows and to frame the doorways down to the floor, where the baseboard (also flat stock) travels horizontally around the room, masking the seam between the walls and

It's All in the Details

White wood trim, a classic choice in Bungalow kitchens from their earliest days, is used in this brand-new kitchen in an old-fashioned way but with fresh, contemporary results. Not only is the trim elegant and decorative but it also knits all the disparate aspects of this kitchen together, creating an integrated yet lively whole.

For example, the door casing and the refrigerator casing stand side by side (see photo at right), but rather than treat each frame separately, one long head casing and a wide center casing tie the two together. (To visually equalize the height of the openings, the owner devised the ingenious wine rack over the refrigerator.) The trim around the breakfast nook and the pantry door (see photo on the facing page) is dealt with in a similar way.

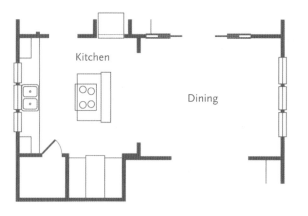

Kitchen

Dining

The language of trim

Decorative trim has a vocabulary all its own, and it's useful to know the meaning of these terms, as they might be used in the Arts and Crafts and Bungalow setting.

Beadboard: A type of woodwork featuring thin strips of wood bordered with fine beading.

Capital: The head, top, or crown of a column.

Chair rail: A strip of wood that runs around the perimeter of a room, often a dining room, usually about 3 ft. or 4 ft. from the floor, representing the place where most chairs rest against the wall.

Column: A supporting pillar that includes a base at the bottom and a capital at the top. In Bungalows, columns are almost always made of wood. These are seen on porches as supports for the roof and in archways between interior rooms.

Crown molding: The wood trim that runs around the top of a room between the ceiling and the walls.

Dado: The lower part of an interior wall, especially one that is decorated. In Bungalows, dadoes are typically wood or a combination of wood and plaster.

Door casing: The wood trim that surrounds a doorway.

Head casing: The wood trim at the top of a doorway.

Plank, planking: A type of flat, rough wood, used in Bungalow kitchens as a rustic wall covering.

Plate rail: A rail or narrow shelf, about 5 ft. to 6 ft. above the floor, used to hold plates or other decorative objects.

Wainscot: A wooden lining for an interior wall. Often it is the height of a chair rail, but occasionally it is the height of a plate rail. It is usually finished differently from the rest of the wall.

the floors. Small details like having the head casings extend out a little longer than the width of the side casings adds a solid Arts and Crafts touch.

A second trim technique is to use a very Bungalow/Craftsman/Arts and Crafts method, which is to apply flat stock wood casing around the doors, windows, and built-ins that might interrupt the walls of the kitchen. The head casing of the windows then travels horizontally around the room linking the tops of the doors and windows, and creates a datum that links the walls of the kitchen together. The space above this trim is a classic location for painted friezes, stencil patterns, wallpaper, or painted fields that are different from the lower walls.

Adding a chair rail can create another trim element that is lower on the wall, although chair rails at the height of the back of a chair was already seen as passé in the Bungalow period, a part of the now out-of-date Victorian style.

When you have wood paneling, as was so common at the turn of the 20th century, a common method for protecting the walls is to install picture rail molding, which is a small crown molding fixed just below the ceiling. When hanging artwork, for example, metal clips are slipped over the picture rail and the wires that support the picture are left exposed against the wall, an effect that is appropriate to the Bungalow style.

Perhaps more relevant to a kitchen or an adjacent dining area is the use of a plate rail, which is similar to a picture rail, although the molding is wider, allowing it to be used as a narrow shelf to display decorative plates or small baubles.

The "dining room" style of trim, as well as the lower chair rail and beadboard dado, can look great in a Bungalow kitchen and are part of the larger Bungalow vocabulary you can draw upon to create your new space. In transitional houses, where the kitchen may have been updated into a Bungalow or Arts and Crafts style, it can be fun to incorporate some of the elements of the older style that may prevail elsewhere in the house. Creating harmony and unity of styles through the trim system is an effective way to integrate a Bungalow kitchen into an older-style house or to flavor the look of a kitchen in new construction.

Trimwork, materials, and color are effective ways to connect rooms visually. A California Bungalow kitchen flows easily into the dining area via wood flooring and flat trimwork.

4 | OUT OF THE BOX: CABINETRY, COUNTERS, AND BUILT-INS

Cabinetry is the star of any kitchen and in no place more so than the Bungalow kitchen. In original Bungalows, the cabinetry was always useful but often rather plain. Kitchen furniture generally consisted of shelves, a worktable, and maybe a Hoosier cabinet, all serviceable but not very sophisticated. Even in the later Bungalows of the 1920s and '30s when cabinets began to be planned and built-in, they were often simply painted with glossy white paint. As the years passed and appliances got bigger and bulkier, original Bungalow kitchens began to appear a little awkward.

(Facing page) This well-proportioned kitchen island, a late 20th-century concoction, holds a commanding position in the kitchen, essentially replacing the original Bungalow-style kitchen worktable. It provides a prep surface, serving space, clean-up area, beverage refrigerator, and storage.

(Above) Antique Arts and Crafts tile accent a field of subway tile to create a customized backsplash for a new Bungalow kitchen.

The bracket that supports the cabinet eases the transition from the upper cabinet to the base below with its soft yet solid curve. Such handcrafted cabinetry detail is one hallmark of the Bungalow style.

In today's Bungalow kitchens, the beautiful woodwork that characterized the more formal rooms of original Bungalows is brought into the kitchen. Attractive Arts and Crafts tile and metalwork, once seen only in the living room of a Bungalow, is now visible throughout the kitchen, the casual dining spaces, and the Bungalow-style family rooms. Of course, glamorous state-of-the-art appliances are also part of the Bungalow kitchen, but now instead of appearing out of place, they fit right in—sometimes literally.

No doubt as you've been considering the floor plan that you want and need; what your new floor, walls, and ceiling will look like; and the placement of your windows and doors, the topic of the cabinetry is probably lurking in your mind, perhaps front and center. As I've said, the cabinetry in the kitchen is not only the most visible aspect of any kitchen but also usually the most expensive purchase when renovating an old kitchen or building a new one. You want it to look beautiful, but you don't want to go bankrupt creating it. And most of all, since you're putting together a Bungalow-style kitchen, you want it to be appropriate—up to date yet evocative of its history.

First, it's important to clarify that "cabinetry" is not simply the kitchen cabinets that line the walls, although certainly those cabinets are essential. One might say that cabinetry consists of all the architectural elements that are permanently attached to the floor or walls. This includes not only upper and lower cabinets and counters but also shelving, tall cupboards (once known as broom closets), other storage elements, and possibly a breakfast nook. In the language of the Bungalow kitchen (and in our modern lexicon), cabinetry may also include an island, a peninsula, a desk (or even a small office), and possibly a media center. In old and new kitchens, cabinetry also includes backsplashes, countertops, and a variety of decorative elements.

Cabinetry

As with most early American styles, original Bungalow kitchens had simple cabinetry that was more utilitarian then decorative in nature. With the kitchen often located behind closed doors at the back of the house, the fancy woodwork with the formal rooms literally stopped at the kitchen, and for the sake of economy, much simpler finish details were used in the kitchen.

A built-in boot bench located by the back door to the kitchen becomes part of the half-wall separating the area from the adjacent family space. Attached to a built-in desk, the bench further establishes the integrated look of the room.

Stainless steel, prized in restaurant kitchens for its easy-to-clean durability, is consistent with the Bungalow tradition of functional beauty. Here, the slick surface contrasts nicely with the cherry cabinetry.

Today's Bungalow kitchens are highly integrated with the rest of the house and present the perfect opportunity to play up more interesting or lavish woodwork that was once visible only in the more formal rooms. On the other hand, it's important to make sure that there is visual continuity between your kitchen and the adjoining spaces. Some say that with cabinetry, the imagination should be allowed to dance with the past, meaning that we should take the opportunity to revive concepts of early Bungalow design. Along with the materials we chose, cabinetry is at the heart of the Bungalow style.

Box Basics

Kitchen cabinetry can be divided into three types: upper cabinets, lower cabinets (or base units), and freestanding islands. Lower units and islands support the work surfaces that are covered by countertops. Convention

The built-in shelving (above) separates the kitchen from the family room. With kitchen cabinets on the other side, the working peninsula (facing page) is tied together with a stone countertop and rounded, white shelves that evoke Bungalow kitchens of the 1930s.

SEEING THE LIGHT OF DAY

A clever device for getting more light into a kitchen along a wall that otherwise would be given over to a solid mass of wood cabinetry is to incorporate an inoperable window behind the upper cabinet, face it with a glass door, and then simply allow the daylight to shine through the window and the cabinet into the room. (Just be sure you include objects in the cabinet that you don't mind displaying.)

This same idea can be used in reverse when struggling to find cabinet space in an old Bungalow kitchen. Many original Bungalows featured small windows high up on a wall, for example. Simply build a glass-fronted cabinet over the window. In a larger window, consider fitting glass shelves to the size of the window.

holds that counter height is 36 in. above the finished floor and that upper cabinets are 18 in. above the countertops.

Fitted cabinetry has more of the appearance of integrally linked base units and corresponding upper cabinets, while unfitted cabinetry takes on more of the appearance of separate pieces that were gathered together over time and assembled into a working whole where the finishes are less uniform, and the overall effect is more informal, or "country" looking. Both fitted and unfitted styles can be used to good effect in a Bungalow kitchen. Unfitted cabinets are more closely associated with the first period of Bungalow construction when the concept of the modern kitchen was still being developed By the second period in the 1920s and '30s, most kitchens were taking on a more familiar appearance, similar to the fitted kitchens we see in most houses today.

A mix of "found" cabinets, furniture pieces, and built-in elements gives this kitchen the look of one from an early Bungalow. New base cabinetry was designed to match the look of the upper cabinets, which the owner salvaged from local sources.

A fresh take on the old-fashioned butler's pantry, elegant cabinets form a functional break between the kitchen and the dining room. Space between the upper and lower cabinets creates a sight line between the two rooms as well as a useful pass-through. The glass doors on either side allow light to shine through and highlight the contents of the cabinet.

The ribbed glass panels on these custom cabinet doors lighten the look of a bank of cabinetry yet obscure the practical (as opposed to ornamental) contents within. Even stock cabinets can have interesting art-glass patterns added to create a unique, period-style touch.

Stock Cabinets

The most basic and least expensive way to buy cabinetry is in stock configurations of base units, uppers, islands, and assorted pantry, desk, and storage units that are available in sizes that can be varied usually in increments of 2 in. to 6 in. in width. Base units are almost always made to be 36 in. high, and uppers are available in depths of 12 in. and heights between 24 in. and 36 in. The cost for making these units is low because they are mass-produced, but they are available in such a variety that mixing and matching the manufactured components to create a customized look is not difficult, especially when the right countertop material is chosen.

Because the Bungalow style is so popular these days, many manufacturers are making cabinetry that fits the basic parameters of the Arts and Crafts styles, such as glass-fronted cabinets with paned windows; designs hinting at Mission or Prairie antecedents; and the use of oak or cherry veneers that reflect early Bungalow styles. However, as with everything, "the devil is in the details," so proportion and choice of materials are critical.

In the Arts and Crafts style craftsmanship is key. The continuous horizontal wood grain across the entire cherry base-unit drawers produces a dramatic design that proudly displays the piece's high-quality workmanship.

REMOVABLE DRAWERS

Original Arts and Crafts style houses were filled with clever devices, some designed for the sake of beauty, others for the sake of practicality. This convenient system of removable cabinet drawers stays true to its Bungalow-style heritage on both accounts. The handsome boxes slide into slots and appear to be ordinary drawers. However, they can be pulled out, and carried off for any number of purposes, like toolboxes. The owner of this kitchen uses them for small cooking implements but they could also easily hold table cutlery, houseplant equipment, or any other materials that might require their own portable holder.

A work of art, these glorious oak cabinets feature carefully chosen wood veneers with strong running grain patterns, which are so prominent that they are the decoration on otherwise plain wooden boxes. Only the highest-quality cuts of wood are designated veneer grade.

Stock cabinetry is the least expensive and can often be made of cheap particleboard that will begin to deteriorate with exposure to moisture. Hardware on stock cabinetry is often of low quality, and particleboard does not hold screws and other fasteners for very long.

Semicustom Cabinetry

If your budget can stand it, it is a sound idea to move up to the next category of quality when selecting your cabinetry: semicustom cabinetry. This is the middle category in the price scale, and the quality of construction and design makes a healthy jump upward.

Most manufacturers use hardwood plywood construction for the carcases (or basic shelf boxes) of their cabinets and use significantly better veneers on the outsides. For the sake of stability and durability, most quality cabinetry uses hardwood plywood for the boxes and doors and nice veneers on the surface. Ironically, solid planks of wood are less stable in high-humidity areas like kitchens and actually don't hold up as well as veneered surfaces.

Semicustom cabinetry shares some of the cost-saving benefits of mass production but is available in greater variations, so the cabinets can be fitted to specific spaces without the use of filler strips to make up the difference. Hence, the label "semicustom." Also, manufacturers will address such details as making counter heights more responsive to individual taste.

With the higher cost and better quality of this cabinetry category, you get more attention to detail and design. Here you stand a far greater chance of finding cabinetry that really gets the flavor of Bungalow style in its choice of materials, proportions, and finishes.

The more informed you are about the specifics of the Bungalow style in general and of the kitchen you are creating, the happier you will be with your final result. For example, if you are renovating a kitchen in an early

The leaded glasswork on the set of cherry upper cabinets makes a subtle Arts and Crafts statement that reflects the early Bungalow-style period and yet has a modern look.

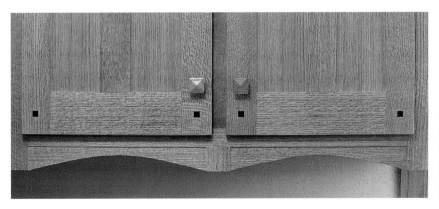

The curved valance, square walnut pegs in the door stiles, and shaped wood pulls on these cabinet doors are classic Arts and Crafts touches that make a powerful impact when they are used throughout the kitchen.

To blend old cabinetry with new in a renovated kitchen, the cabinetmaker created lower cabinets to match. To support the upper cabinets, whimsical columns in a similar classic style were added.

20th-century Bungalow, you'll want to research the type of wood used throughout the rest of the house and select cabinetry that is similar if not the same. If you are building a new kitchen in the Bungalow style, study up on the variations of the style (Arts and Crafts, Mission, Prairie), and make choices in cabinetry consistent with the historic precedents of that style. Chances are good that you can find semicustom cabinetry that will work well.

Custom Cabinetry

Of course, the best way to get the cabinetry that you really want is to have it custom built. If budget permits, with custom cabinetry, a host of options become available to you. For starters, if you live in an original Bungalow, you may decide to open up your kitchen to the original formal dining room. Turning a cabinetmaker loose on creating a set of kitchen cabinets that respect and/or duplicate design details in your Bungalow's original woodwork can be absolutely thrilling, for the architect, the artisans, and for you—and completely in keeping with the style of the house. Or, you might find existing cabinetry components, such as an antique counter or old armoire, at a salvage yard or antique dealer and want to incorporate it into your new kitchen. If you are going the custom route, these pieces can be tied in to your kitchen's cabinetry in inventive ways. Also, bear in mind that these creative notions can sometimes work exceptionally well with stock and semicustom cabinetry, too.

Generally, natural wood finish cabinets relate more to the first period of Bungalow design, whereas painted cabinets relate to the second. But there's no law that says you can't mix finishes, where a blend of painted

Painted, curved cabinetry evokes the Bungalow style of the 1930s. The curved end of a base cabinet provides a space for cookbooks while softening the passageway to the nearby butler's pantry.

Finding original themes that appear in glass, woodwork, or flooring in other rooms throughout your Bungalow and bringing them into your new kitchen can be an effective design concept—and a lot of fun, too. Here, a stylized "tree of life" pattern done in leaded glass adorns all the upper cabinets in this renovated kitchen of a 1906 Bungalow. The pattern was adapted from a piece of original built-in cabinetry in the house's dining room.

Details from Details

MORGAN STANDARDIZED MOULDINGS

After wrestling with the many decisions necessary to complete a major renovation of her kitchen, this owner needed to find decorative brackets to support the new upper cabinets. She had worked with her architect on everything from space planning to choosing the correct stone for her countertops, and now she wanted something special for the brackets under the cabinets. Although this was a small detail, it was a signature one.

Many sources are readily available for inspiration for such decisions, including reprints of old millwork, furniture, and cabinet catalogs from the Bungalow era (see bottom left), not to mention scores of magazine and book photographs of both new and period kitchens.

The perfect solution was found in a tiny built-in china cabinet in the original breakfast room (above), which adjoins the kitchen. The supports for the two shelves in the cabinet actually appear to be small valances, but the owner could visualize each as a pair of horizontal brackets connected at their tails. She traced the profile of what would become a single bracket on a piece of paper and then asked her architect to scale it to the size necessary to support the larger upper cabinets in the kitchen. Wood brackets were then created from the pattern. The new kitchen now reflects a lovely piece of history from the original house.

The dark-stained oak used in this cabinet is quintessentially Bungalow style, evoking Mission-style furniture. The seeded glass in the cabinet doors adds further to the handmade feel.

surfaces can provide visual relief in a room heavy with dark wood. Dark stained oak is the most prevalent material for Bungalow cabinets because that wood was commonly used in formal rooms of these houses. Cherry can also work well in a Bungalow kitchen because it has a warm, distinctive grain and color that blends well with the Arts and Crafts aesthetic. The darker woods with prominent grain fit the style better than light woods such as maple and birch. Pine is generally too soft and associated with country- or Colonial-style cabinetry to feel right in a Bungalow.

After dining areas and family rooms, an office space is one of the most common requests in a Bungalow-style kitchen. Here, a substantial cherry desk and tall bookcase are balanced and lightened by a painted kitchen storage unit, vertical paned windows, and a French door leading to the deck.

Cabinetry need not be brown or white to work in the Bungalow vernacular. Here, celery green vertical-plank cabinets bring color and whimsy to a kitchen fitted with butcher-block countertops and a jet black soapstone sink.

A rich mahogany countertop harkens back to the formal butler's pantries in late Victorian and early Bungalow homes. The chocolate brown wood is offset by the white base cabinetry and eggshell blue on the walls.

Countertops

Countertops and backsplashes are another great place to draw on the Arts and Crafts vocabulary. Many types of materials make great choices for a Bungalow kitchen. Remember, however, that the Bungalow aesthetic is all about natural materials and handmade, well-crafted elements. A chrome and black lacquer counter might look great in an Art Deco house but would be too slick looking and out of place in a Bungalow kitchen. Instead, historically correct elements, such as wood, tile, and metal, make excellent choices. Also, down-to-earth craftsman elements like terrazzo can also work beautifully, not because they were ever used originally but because they reflect the warmth and artistry of the period.

Wooden Counters

The wooden countertops used as work surfaces in early Bungalows are an excellent choice for today. Butcher-block maple and cherry wood counters can work and blend well with darker oak cabinetry. And butcher block stands up well to water and abuse and has an appropriate functional look. Mahogany is the countertop material of choice for many Bungalow kitchens. Although mahogany can appear a bit too rich for use throughout an entire kitchen, it can be an elegant option for an island or coupled with stone or tile on counters. Mahogany was commonly used in the butler's pantries in Victorian-era homes and adds a period touch in a Bungalow.

Handcrafted tile makes for a richly textured countertop and backsplash. To soften the counter's edge, cream-colored bull-nosed tile was used so that the entire piece is one material. A single dragonfly tile adds to the counter's custom feel.

If you choose wood for a counter, remember that wood counters are easy to damage, so unless you want to use them like butcher block, where you literally use the surface to cut on, you might want to select something else for your more active and wet areas. Wood needs to be treated about once a year with oil to seal the grain against water and dirt, or sealed with a semigloss polyurethane coating. Wood strip flooring can also be used as a countertop material, and since it has a more rustic appearance, it looks particularly appropriate in smaller kitchens incorporating elements of early Bungalow style.

A stainless-steel counter with its integrated sink basin and back-splash has a decidedly contemporary industrial look but works well in a Bungalow setting, especially when it is combined with period-style tile and hardware.

TIME GONE BY

Equipped with an array of devices such as a flour bin and sifter, a sugar bin, a spice wheel, a silverware drawer, a bread drawer, and cupboard space for dishes, pots, and pans, a Hoosier cabinet was usually a stepback cupboard made of oak with a porcelain or tin work surface.

Produced by The Hoosier Manufacturing Company of New Castle, Indiana, which was in business from 1898 (or 1903) to 1935, Hoosiers were considered to be the ultimate household convenience. Today, they are popular collectibles that fit comfortably in any Bungalow kitchen, old or new.

HOOSIER
the Kitchen Cabinet that saves miles of steps

"The Hoosier will help me to stay young"

"RETAIN your youthful energy and girlish appearance," is the wedding-day advice of thousands of mothers. As they look back over the years, they realize that woman's charms soon fade and her health often gives way when drudgery methods rule her days.

But in Hoosier homes, daughters know the miles of needless steps and hours of wasted time that this scientific kitchen helper saves. They honor it for the service it has rendered the "little Mother" who has been able to give more freely of her time to a happy comradeship with her children.

The bride from a Hoosier home will have a Hoosier.

It will be numbered among thoughtful wedding gifts or be first on her list of household needs. Other brides should know what the Hoosier means. And millions of tired Mothers should also learn how the Hoosier reduces kitchen work and frees them from burdensome labor.

The Hoosier merchant is anxious to demonstrate this automatic servant. Will you go and see the many models now? Also send to us for "New Kitchen Short Cuts"—a book every housewife should have.

If you don't know the name of the local Hoosier store, be sure to ask us.

SET IN STONE

Terrazzo is a composite of masonry material and broken bits of marble or other hard stone that is combined into a concrete slurry, hardened, poured, then polished to a high gloss. Historically, terrazzo was used for flooring, but in recent years, it has been used effectively—and economically—for countertops. The advantage of such a process is that the counter can be formed to suit any shape and is often made on site on top of the finished cabinet bases.

Although terrazzo was not used in original Bungalow kitchens, it works beautifully in new ones because of its Arts and Crafts sensibility.

In addition to bits of broken marble or other stone, the concrete slurry can contain any sort of rock, broken glass or crockery, or even special found objects. Concrete also takes color well, so it can be dyed to suit any color scheme. This terrazzo countertop was created with recycled glass from old stoplights, giving it a unique, multifaceted sense of light and color.

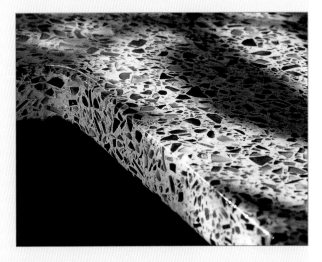

Tile Counters

Tile is a classic Arts and Crafts material that can make a particularly beautiful counter. Tile, including faience, subway tiling, and Arts and Crafts illustrative tiles, are incredibly handsome, either singly or combined with each other or with wood trims. They are also historically very much part of the original Bungalow aesthetic.

The problem with tile is that it is less practical than wood, metal, or other countertop options. The most beautiful tiles are irregular in shape and need to be set in a thick grout. Both the rough surface of the tile and the grout tend to absorb stains and are difficult to keep clean. Using tile in a Bungalow kitchen is a great choice but perhaps better on a backsplash or on a wall space that sees less activity than a countertop.

Metal Counters

Metal countertops are another option, with materials like copper and stainless steel offering both a contemporary industrial look as well as a hint of the past. Copper and tin have a real precedent in the Bungalow style, having been commonly used on Hoosier cabinets and other kitchen surfaces. Copper, however, needs to be either sealed with a coating that keeps it from oxidizing, or polished as necessary if you don't want it to darken to a brownish color. Stainless steel, when glued down tight to a wooden substrate, can have an old-fashioned appearance. When the metal is folded over the edges of the counter and molded into the sink basin, the whole assembly becomes easy to work on and, because there are no seams, easy to clean.

Terrazzo and Concrete Counters

Terrazzo is made up of crushed marble and other stones mixed into a concrete slurry, poured, allowed to harden, and then polished to a high gloss. Terrazzo can be beautiful on a counter, takes color well, and can include small keepsakes like coins and rings to be mixed in for special effect. Poured concrete is also a possibility; after all, it is a raw material, and it can be formed and poured to fit any configuration. It can also be tinted any color, stained, and polished to a sheen that rivals that of any stone counter.

This green limestone slab counter offers a modern counterpoint to the old-fashioned open shelving. It has a matte finish that allows the beautiful texture of the stone to show through without distracting reflections.

Other Solid-Surface Counters

Marble, granite, terrazzo, and even synthetic stone materials make practical and beautiful kitchen counters. Some of these substances have historic precedents (marble, for example) but many are new.

Serpentine. Serpentine has a greenish tint and has beautiful grain pattern. It is softer than granite but harder than marble, which is more porous and stains easily. Carrara marble was commonly used in the late 19th and early 20th centuries as a sink and counter material. Of course, today it's still used for pastry-preparation surfaces.

Granite and marble. Granite and marble tile can be purchased in squares about half an inch thick and is so uniform in dimension that the grout lines are wire thin between them. Because they sit so flat, the tiles seem like a solid surface. They need a wood edge to trim them off, but this can be a nice accent.

The muted grays of the Carrara marble countertop work well with the soft hues of the cabinetry, without competing with the bold backsplash tile.

This countertop marks the ingenious use of 12-in. black granite floor tile at a cost that is far less than a slab of the same material. The edges of the tiles are so crisp and even that they fit together without grout and are finished off with a walnut wood edge treatment, reflecting the cabinetry.

HONING

Honing is a process of treating or "sanding off" the slick surface of a stone counter to create a matte finish on the stone. Honing, which can be done on any stone surface, goes a long way toward achieving a more "natural" surface.

Although honing was not a process used in original Bungalow countertops, its natural appearance on stone counters blends well with the Bungalow style. For example, when black granite is honed, the surface ends up very much like natural slate yet without slate's vulnerability to scratching and staining. Remember, honed countertops should be sealed about once a year.

Honed black marble has much of the same appearance of slate but is much more durable. A popular choice for counters, granite is available in many colors and grain configurations that can work well in the Arts and Crafts domain. Although granite is the hardest of the stones, it, too, needs to be sealed against stains. The slab stones work well for undermount-style sinks, where there is no rim to catch your sponge on and spills and crumbs can be easily swept into the sink.

Slate. Black slate has texture and depth but stains easily and needs to be sealed every year or two. Slate is a historic-looking material when used for countertops and sinks because as it ages, its patina becomes deeper.

Rather than having a grooved surface with tapered slots for this built-in stone drainboard, the countertop itself is angled toward the sink to provide a smooth and sanitary drainage system.

A common treatment in original Bungalow kitchens, the backsplash in this rustic kitchen is kept to a minimum height and is made of the same wood as the countertop.

FOOL THE EYE

A solid slab of stone, 1½ in. thick, will have a more substantial appearance than one only ¾-in. thick, the standard dimension of many slabs used for kitchen counters. Many species of stone can be ordered in the thicker dimension but, naturally, at a significant increase in cost. A great way to give the appearance of a thicker slab of stone is to laminate the edge of a counter with a second piece of ¾-in. stone, which looks very close to the real item.

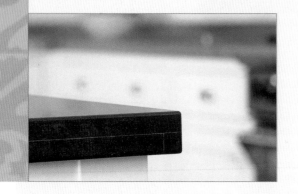

Synthetic stone. Synthetic stone counters like Corian® continue to improve in appearance, but they are still "plastic." There's something about this material in a Bungalow that isn't quite right, but these materials usually cost less than real stone, and their edges can be shaped in attractive profiles, just like real stone.

Backsplashes

Backsplashes are used to decorate and protect the wall just above the countertop and to seal the joint between the back of the countertop and the wall. In purely functional terms, backsplashes don't need to be much higher than 3 in. to 4 in. to do the trick, but unless you are really on a budget or have a particularly interesting wall to showcase, the backsplash is an opportunity to have fun with color and pattern and to provide an artistic focus for the kitchen, especially with Arts and Crafts tile.

Commercially available Arts and Crafts tiles that are replicas of old, traditional tiles, such as simple faience or more decorative designs, look right at home in today's Bungalow kitchen.

Beauty and function unite for a dramatic tile back-splash. The scene created by the mosaic tile makes reference to a river landscape that is part of the view outside the windows of the kitchen.

A rule of thumb is to use the same material as the counter for the backsplash if you are keeping your backsplash to a minimum height. However, if the backsplash is going to be more than 4 in., consider doing something creative with tile, wood, or stone.

Caring for a backsplash requires the same attention as attending to a kitchen counter. Grout between tiles can get dirty, either with cooking splatters, mildew, or everyday grime, and can be hard to clean. Wood needs care too, and it is vulnerable to flame and excessive heat. Smooth stone is easy to care for but can look overwhelming when it is the same material as the counter if your backsplash is higher than 6 in. (An exception might be Cararra marble, which is a material that is used for pastry surfaces in many kitchens and has a long history of use in 19th- and early 20th-century houses as a bathroom vanity top and for kitchen counters.)

Islands and Peninsulas

Modern islands and peninsulas have their Bungalow precedent in the kitchen worktable. In fact, they are often used today in much the same way, providing both work and eating surface. Islands can be perfect spaces to serve a meal or a snack in a pinch, feed the kids, and provide a social gathering station for family and friends to participate in the kitchen activities without getting in the way. Because islands are attached to the floor, they can be wired for electricity to provide outlets and a useful home for stoves, microwaves, and other appliances. They also can be plumbed for sinks and dishwashers, making them a great food-serving and clean-up area, which frees up the rest of the counter space in the kitchen for food preparation.

Islands pose convenient solutions for making use of wasted floor space in many Bungalow kitchens where the main work counters are arranged around the outside of the room. By adding an island, a new work area is created between the counters.

A small border through the field tile follows a step pattern that adds color and dimension.

Kitchen style should reflect your personal style. The owners put their personal stamp on the kitchen by using a favorite motif—the eucalyptus leaf—as a handcrafted border on the backsplash.

The graceful curve in this island eases the passage from the dining area to the family room. With its furniture-style base, this island hints at the old-fashioned kitchen table, but the sleek, black top adds an exciting design touch to this new Bungalow kitchen.

The design of a new island should take its cue from the Bungalow ethic of beautiful functionality and can be either directly related to the design of the overall cabinetry in the kitchen or provide a contrast.

Islands can provide useful storage capacity, especially on the end. This clever use of space, particularly when it is done in an aesthetically pleasing manner, is entirely within the context of the Bungalow and Arts and Crafts ethos.

Furniture-Style Built-ins

Technically, built-ins are pieces of furniture that are attached to the walls or floor of the kitchen. They are different from a finished bookcase or an armoire that is just screwed to the wall; a true built-in piece would be incomplete if it were removed from the wall. For example, at the turn of the 20th century, china cabinets were often installed with their finished front exposed into the kitchen or the dining room but were nailed or screwed to the wall, which served as the back.

An antique display cabinet from an old general store gets a new life as a kitchen island. The owner of this kitchen had the case modified by a carpenter to serve its new function with grace and style.

With its door open wide, a granite-topped island shows off its large storage capacity. The rest of the island provides a home for a convection oven and plenty more storage.

Affordable built-ins

Since built-ins, including benches, bookshelves, armoires, and other cabinets, are such an integral part of the feel of a Bungalow, they are a desirable addition to a Bungalow-style kitchen if you have the space. When working with stock or even semicustom cabinets, ready-made built-ins that are companionable with these cabinets are almost impossible to find. Benches and bookcases are sometimes available, but by definition, built-ins are made to fit specific spaces and therefore are custom creations. They are also usually expensive.

One relatively economical solution is to use stock or semicustom cabinetry for cost savings but splurge by having a carpenter create built-ins to match the cabinetry. Matching wood species can be tricky, so pay attention to color and grain pattern in choosing your materials. If you decide on painted cabinetry, touch-up paint can be ordered from most cabinet manufacturers and be used to paint your built-ins.

Typical of those found in turn-of-the-20th-century builder's catalogs, a built-in china cabinet serves as a display case for one of the owner's many collections. A site-built piece, this built-in requires that the wall it fits into holds it together.

A beautifully executed new breakfast nook resides in a 1916 Sears Ashmore Bungalow. The original plans for the house showed a smaller version of this nook that had been removed long before the current owners renovated the kitchen.

The Breakfast Nook

A popular and characteristic piece in the Bungalow style is the breakfast nook. Most traditional breakfast nooks consisted of a built-in tabletop and bench seats mounted in an alcove, ideally on an east-facing outside wall to catch morning sun. Nooks were and are great gathering spots, homework centers, and cozy reading areas that allow noncooks to be in the kitchen without getting in the way.

A close cousin to the breakfast nook is banquette seating, ideally located in a corner of a room. The seating is built in to the walls, and a freestanding table is positioned in front of it. During mealtimes, the table can be pulled out to accommodate diners, but when not in use the table can be pushed in, like tucking a chair under a table to make more room. The table for the banquette is often built to be a companion for the benches. On the other hand, it can be a found piece used like any other piece of furniture in the room.

BUNGALOW STYLE

NOOK NOTES

Where the classic original breakfast nook was designed with a pair of benches facing each other across the table, in the new Bungalow kitchen, the idea can be reconsidered in a multitude of ways. For example, instead of two benches, you could have three, or perhaps just one that wraps around three sides.

Also, instead of conventional solid, hard seats, benches can take upholstered cushions or might be built using wooden slats that give the benches a slightly springy, more cushioned feel. By the way, under each of the three bench sections on this arrangement is a "crumb-catcher shelf" that slides out like the tray at the bottom of a toaster oven for easy cleaning.

This breakfast nook is composed of an angled banquette with a table built to be a companion to the benches. Located in the corner, classic two-over-one windows flood this pleasant space with light and bring in views.

The built-in style of bench seating that makes a banquette can be also used as a cozy spot to perch in the kitchen. Sometimes it's nice just to have a place to sit and take it all in. An interesting hybrid of the banquette seating area can include another common built-in feature, the bookcase. The wood so characteristic of the Bungalow style can be carried over from the kitchen cabinetry and pressed into service as a combination library and informal dining area.

Though the kitchen lacked an eating nook, the owners were able to create an informal dining area in a space that was once an enclosed porch.

A necessary convenience for most kitchens is a desk space. The new version here fits well within the Bungalow vocabulary with its built-in appearance, dark oak wood, and heavy proportions.

Kitchen Offices

Another functional built-in that can be effective in a Bungalow-style kitchen is a desk area. There aren't many historic precedents for kitchen office spaces, but they can be designed to look like they really belong and allow for yet another function in the kitchen. It's a way to extend the use of the Arts and Crafts-style woodwork throughout the kitchen and provide a desirable place to put the phone and message center, the home computer, and even keys, mail, and many other small household necessities.

Having a large home office is a real luxury (facing page). This desk and office storage cabinet with charming cubby drawers (above) are made of the same stained oak as the wood trim in the rest of the house. They serve as both a break between the kitchen and the family room as well as a focal point that ties the rooms together.

Storage Problems Solved

Storage in any kitchen is always an issue, and in a Bungalow kitchen it's even more so. Creating places to keep things in a way that doesn't look forced can be a challenge in small spaces. However, many people have found elegant solutions for tucking away kitchen necessities that are perfectly in keeping with the Bungalow style.

Ingenious opportunities for storage can be found just about anywhere in or near the kitchen, and sometimes the subtlest rethinking of a common storage problem—or a small area—provides an ideal solution. For example, that overhead cupboard where you store the Belgian waffle iron you use twice a year can actually be turned into a roll-out drawer that lets you gain easy access to the contents without standing on a stool.

These inventive roll-out drawers provide lots of convenient storage in a new butler's pantry adjacent to the kitchen. Although the drawers are 21st-century inventions, they are very much in keeping with the Arts and Crafts aesthetic.

Classic Cool (and Dry)

This "breather box" is a piece of historic ingenuity, which borrows from the milk-delivery boxes that were built into exterior walls in the early part of the 20th century. The idea was to have a box mounted in the outside wall of the house, usually in the kitchen or mudroom porch, that could be opened from the outside so the milkman could drop off his bottles and from the inside by the homeowner to retrieve them.

A useful overhead roll-out drawer allows easy access to items that would otherwise be buried deep in the cabinet, out of sight and out of mind.

The "Swiss Army Knife" of Cabinetry

One of the architects I interviewed for this book referred to the island in his kitchen as the "Swiss Army knife" of cabinetry. Like a Swiss Army knife that ingeniously conceals not only a pocketknife but also a screwdriver, scissors, a nail file, a bottle opener, a key ring—and whatever else—this island cleverly includes kitchen appliances, storage, seating, and workspace.

On the "business" side of the island, which faces the work area of the kitchen, is a convenient bar sink, a microwave oven, and plenty of storage space. (Incidentally, a microwave positioned in a unique low position is great in households with children; they can heat up food for themselves without risking injury by climbing on counters.) On the "customer" side of the island, family and friends can pull up a stool and have a quick meal, a drink, or just engage in conversation with the cook. The butcher-block countertop helps make food preparation a cinch, and it overhangs just enough so knees can be tucked under while sitting on the stools. More storage is included on this side as well, hidden behind tall cupboard doors.

A special feature of this island is the built-in china cabinet on the end. Styled like a piece of furniture, it gives the whole room a strong Arts and Crafts feeling. The wood finish of the cabinet nestles up against the painted finish of the rest of the island and makes

a great union of the two finishes, which, in turn, are used elsewhere in the kitchen and adjacent family room. The china cabinet is taller than the rest of the island, which forms a wall to keep things from falling off that end of the countertop and also hides from view the more utilitarian aspects of the island.

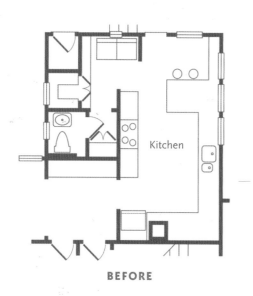

BEFORE

Mudroom

Pantry

Kitchen/
family room

AFTER

Shelves need not be deep to be useful. These small shelves, tucked in an out-of-the-way corner, snugly hold some essential pantry items.

Pantry storage is a study unto itself, but the underlying principle is that if the pantry storage is deeper than one can of food, what ends up behind that can is lost. Creating large, flat storage areas for cans, bottles, boxes of cereal, and other food staples is important in kitchen layout. This notion can be achieved by placing flat-paneled doors across a shallow wall set back. These doors can relate directly to the other cabinet doors in the kitchen, as well as reflect the warmth of the Bungalow style.

Another type of storage space that is contemporary but still reflects the craftsmanship of the old style is the "exploding" wall cabinet, with layers of folding shelves that stack back together. Also, inclined shelves, close cousins to exploding cabinets, in the drawer make the contents easy to see and reach.

An efficient layered, folding-shelf system allows for lots of shallow shelving in a relatively small area.

A his-and-hers hanging storage space more than does justice to the classic Bungalow-style mudroom. Located just inside the kitchen door, this intelligent system includes overhead storage, a convenient seat, and conceals the heat register in its baseboard.

The Well-Crafted Armoire

Since the Bungalow kitchen often includes a dining area and/or a family room, it may also require storage of a more general type. This is when a built-in armoire, designed to match the kitchen cabinetry, can be both a beautiful and useful addition. It may hold the food processor, the baking equipment, or the Thanksgiving roasting pan, or, in this day and age, it may hold the toner for the computer printer or a state-of-the-art CD player. Regardless of its purpose, an armoire can still bring a Bungalow ethic into the entire space.

Built-ins by the Door

The mudroom, common to many early Bungalows, is one of the first spaces gobbled up for use in the new kitchen. However, every household needs a mudroom, even if it is no longer a room or even an enclosed space. (For more, see Chapter 2.)

Thus, an important storage necessity is a place to hang coats, store boots, hats, and mittens, and perhaps place some other indoor-outdoor items. Built-in storage in entries has evolved much beyond the coat closet. Today, not only is a mudroom built-in a great opportunity to create organized space but a place to show off beautiful woodwork so integral to the Bungalow look.

Nothing says "Bungalow style" more vociferously than woodwork. Remember, in the Bungalow kitchen, woodwork includes not only traditional kitchen cabinets but also islands, armoires, shelving, and other built-in elements that are required for the way we live. As you craft your Bungalow-style kitchen, keep in mind that they need to reflect the quality and craftsmanship of the past, but they should address the practical needs of today.

Every kitchen needs a space nearby to hang coats and store outerwear. This version, located in a hallway just outside the kitchen, is essentially a large Bungalow-style built-in, where the hallway wall is the back of the cabinet.

Floor-to-ceiling storage is a great mudroom luxury. Fitted with reproduction pulls, this built-in storage piece keeps the entryway clean and clear.

5 | THE WORKING KITCHEN: APPLIANCES, FIXTURES, AND GADGETS

Once a new kitchen space is thoughtfully designed and fitted with cabinetry and interior finishes, it's time to add the equipment that will make it function: appliances, fixtures, and other kitchen gadgets. Appliances are those pieces that involve electricity or gas and are the active components in the kitchen. Fixtures, in contrast, are the more static pieces such as sinks and faucets. But no matter the element, in this chapter we'll show you a full range of styles to inspire your designs.

(Facing page) This handsome Magic Chef® range, a 1930s model, was originally designed to use natural gas, and features then-new thermostatic control for the ovens as well as separate burner controls. Surrounded by antique tile, the stove and its colorful accents give the whole room a classic sensibility.

(Above) The white range is an antique, although dating from the 1950s, it's not as old as the kind you would have seen in earlier Bungalows. It has a decidedly retro appearance that isn't entirely true to the era but fits well in the California Craftsman vernacular and brings a strong design focus to the kitchen.

An early 1920s Victory Clarion cookstove is the focal point of a new Bungalow kitchen in a lakeside vacation house. This stove's antique appearance contributes to the comfortable, old-fashioned flavor of the kitchen. A "dual fuel" appliance, it burns wood for the ovens but uses gas for the cooktop. It is also particularly functional in the winter because it throws off extra heat that helps warm the house.

Ranges

There is something elemental about cooking and fire, and ever since humans have been preparing food, the cooking area has been the heart of the home. Because of the duties required of a cooking device, it serves as the center—and often the focal point—of any kitchen. This is no less true in a Bungalow kitchen, original or contemporary.

At the turn of the 20th century, kitchens were often still fitted with woodstoves that served as a combination heat source and cooking tool. However, ranges were fast becoming the norm. Some were fueled with gas or oil; others with electricity. Both were freestanding pieces that included a range top and oven. For fire-prevention reasons, these appliances often needed to stand apart from the rest of the kitchen furnishings, frequently in a discrete nook that was lined with fireproof tile.

Today, a standard range top and oven—whether they are one appliance or not—will occupy a prominent space in the kitchen. When combined with a backsplash and a vent, the whole assembly can become the central design focus of the room.

What Was Out Is In Again

Twenty years ago, a number of manufacturers began marketing "antique" stoves, ranges that look like old-fashioned appliances that were in style in the 1920s and '30s, with furniture-style legs, tall backs, warming ovens, and other period details. Many of these stoves fit beautifully in a new

APPLIANCE APPEAL

When creating a Bungalow-style kitchen, the most basic decision you will make is how you are going to treat new appliances in an old-style room. Here, you have three choices: You can conceal modern fixtures with paneling; you can show them off, using other elements such as cabinetry, lighting, and wall treatments (think wainscoting) to achieve the Bungalow-style look; or you can turn to antique (or reproduction) appliances, particularly old-fashioned ranges and stoves.

It's important to decide which direction you want to take in your new kitchen before you choose appliances because each one's individual appearance and how it appears in relation to the other design elements is important to creating the look.

If you are going to hide your appliances, you need to find ones that can be paneled over or secreted away inside cabinetry. If your appliances are meant to be shown, then you need to choose ones that will be compatible with other elements in the kitchen, particularly the cabinetry.

Commercial-style stoves like this Viking® range are required by code to have a powerful venting system to safely exhaust the heat. The metal tray hanging on the painted beadboard wall behind the range serves as both a decorative element and a protective backsplash.

In addition to refurbished antique ranges, some contemporary ranges have a decidedly retro appearance. This black range is an Italian model that the owners chose for its specific cooking capacities. Its dark color hints at early Bungalow-style ranges.

Bungalow-style kitchen, especially grand 1930s gas stoves painted with enamel in pastel blues or vivid reds.

Heavy-duty commercial ranges are popular these days, especially with serious cooks. They tend to have a more massive look to them that can simulate the style of the original gas or electric ranges. If your budget will allow, these can be a good choice for a new Bungalow-style kitchen.

Contemporary Options

No doubt, including an antique range in your kitchen can enhance the period Bungalow feel, but for many people, the modern stoves offer so many improvements over the old ones that they wouldn't want to go back. These appliances also can be split up, so that the range top can be located in a different place than the ovens, which makes planning its placement in a new kitchen potentially much easier.

BUNGALOW BASICS

Going commercial

Ranges occupied a prominent place in all early kitchens, because of their importance and their size. Today's large commercial-style ranges are not only popular, especially with serious cooks, but also blend well in Bungalow-style kitchens.

Pro-style ranges come in many finishes, but the majority are clad in stainless steel. Stainless or white tend to work best with the Bungalow aesthetic. Most require vent hoods, which were never part of original Bungalow kitchens but can be made compatible with a commercial stove—and the kitchen itself—through the use of like materials. Facing the vent with wood and integrating it with the upper cabinetry is a common solution; designing a metal hood with a patina that complements the range is another.

A striking backsplash, made with Arts and Crafts tile, for example, can also go a long way toward uniting a historic stove with a new vent or even just the stove with the rest of the kitchen.

The Story of a Stove

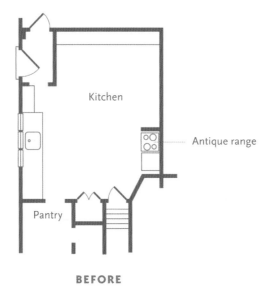

BEFORE

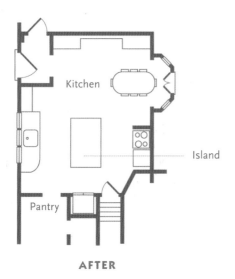

AFTER

Using antique appliances—or reproductions of period-style appliances—in a Bungalow kitchen has a special appeal. Although iceboxes and small gadgets add historical interest, they can rarely used effectively. However, with certain stoves, it's a different story. Not only are they beautiful to look at, but they also can be refurbished and retrofitted to make them effective for safe, everyday cooking.

In this kitchen, the owners chose to revive a 1930s Magic Chef range that was in keeping with their 1930s Bungalow-style kitchen. The stove fit into an existing niche in the interior wall of the kitchen that was lined with original glazed tiles that, in turn, wrapped around the adjacent walls, serving as a beautiful white frame for the handsome green-and-cream-colored range (see p. 169). The range's color was popular for kitchen appliances, bath tiles, and fixtures at the time. To acknowledge the historical accuracy as well as to further highlight the range, the owners painted the kitchen walls a similar shade of pale green.

Several components in the old gas range needed to be brought up to date, including the gas valves, the thermostat mechanism, and the gaskets that sealed the oven doors. The end result is a powerful focal point that perfectly expresses the new Bungalow style.

This vent hood is suspended from the ceiling above a range top located in an island. The hood's stainless-steel finish is softened by the cherry wood column that connects it to the ceiling and also ties it in to the rest of the kitchen, which features cherry cabinetry.

An ultramodern, stainless-steel oven nestles in comfortably with the traditional cherry cabinetry, juxtaposing old and new, which is a hallmark of the new Bungalow kitchen.

Range tops are areas for active cooking, where you are stirring, sautéing, and frying, so placing the cooktop in a more convenient part of the kitchen, or possibly on an island, is often a good solution.

The oven, on the other hand, can be tucked into either an upper or a lower cabinet, a choice that may be dictated by any number of variables. For example, if baking is your passion, you may want your oven to be placed in an area that is close to baking supplies and plenty of counter space for rolling out dough and cooling cakes or cookies.

Coping with Vent Hoods

Vent hoods are virtually a necessity these days, but they have no historic precedent in the home kitchen. Still, they offer another opportunity to interpret the Bungalow style in the modern kitchen.

Vent hoods basically come in two styles: wall hanging or overhead. Wall-hanging vent hoods are often separated from the stove by about 30 in. of wall space that offers yet another opportunity for decoration. In both cases, vents lend themselves to interesting Bungalow-style wood treatments that can tie in visually with the rest of the cabinetry.

Refrigerators

Refrigeration has come a long way from the humble icebox that was a staple in early Bungalow kitchens. Where once the icebox was relegated to a back porch or mudroom, it is now front and center in most kitchens, if only because of its size. It is important to locate this appli-

To accommodate the depth of this Viking cooktop, a base cabinet was designed that is flush with the range but deeper than the surrounding cabinets. Tapered on the sides to "round" the corners, it incorporates deep drawers for pots and pans, resulting in the appearance of a built-in structure. The decorative tile backsplash visually connects the cooktop to the vent hood and creates a dramatic look for the entire kitchen.

COOL CHOICES

SubZero® and other manufacturers make refrigerator drawers, an appliance that can be used effectively in a new Bungalow kitchen. In some kitchens, often a smaller (30-in.) refrigerator is all the space can truly handle, so refrigerator drawers tucked under counters or in an island are a blessing. Also, refrigerator drawers are a good choice if you want to conceal appliances behind panels or other cabinetry. They look just like cabinet drawers when they are closed.

Particularly when placed near informal dining areas or in pantries between the kitchen and the dining room, small under-counter refrigerators can be efficient for storing wine, beverages for kids, or pantry basics. Many of these units often have ice-making capacity, too. Not only is this a convenience at mealtimes, but it also relieves some of the storage demands on the main refrigerator. Like the refrigerator drawers, smaller refrigerators are also easy to conceal with period-style woodwork.

ance where it will be easy to stock; conveniently located counter space for loading and unloading is also a consideration. However, especially in a more modest Bungalow-style kitchen, you don't want the refrigerator to take over the room.

A Matter of Size

The biggest problem with most contemporary refrigerators is that they are so large and, well, contemporary looking. One way to deal with the refrigerator's size is to hide it behind cabinetry. More and more refrigerators are available in "built-in" configurations. These refrigera-

This narrow refrigerator looks like a cupboard, with its paneled fronts that blend into the rest of the cabinetry. The upper section is a refrigerator; the lower, two freezer drawers.

tors come in a 24-in. depth that keeps them from protruding from the face of the cabinetry base units, and then they are paneled with wood that matches the cabinetry, an approach that works well with Bungalow styles. Another solution is to tuck the refrigerator in a found space adjacent to the kitchen, such as a reconfigured pantry or even a closet.

Finally, there is nothing wrong with simply choosing the fridge that offers you the most storage and functionality. Stainless steel is a popular finish these days, and when combined with other stainless-steel appliances like ranges, ovens, and dishwashers the effect is nicely compatible with painted or natural wood finishes. A plain metal finish is more true to the "natural material" ethic of the Bungalow style. Pure white can also be a stunning choice, echoing the simplicity and starkness of the original Bungalow kitchens.

Small Solutions

Increasingly popular refrigerators these days are smaller models, particularly refrigerator drawers and wine refrigerators. Refrigerator drawers fit comfortably in lower cabinets or islands, where they can easily be paneled and disguised. Two drawers in different areas of the kitchen may better serve your needs—and better fit in the kitchen's footprint—than one large appliance.

TIME GONE BY

Introduced in the 1920s, electric refrigeration became every housewife's must-have appliance. Replacing the icebox, the early refrigerator, which featured an enormous compressor fan on top, was actually something of an eyesore. For the first time, food could be kept a consistently cold temperature for much longer periods of time for the steep price of about $400.

Found Space

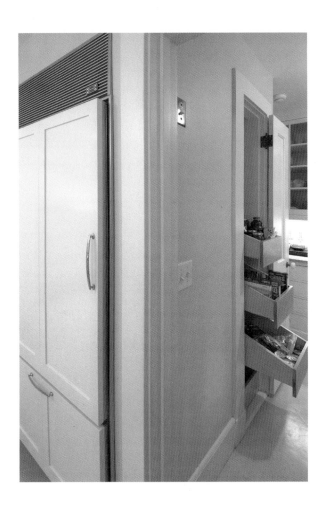

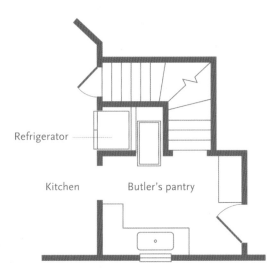

Refrigerator

Kitchen   Butler's pantry

Finding space in an old Bungalow kitchen for large appliances and for storage for the smaller necessities can be a problem. For the owners of this late Bungalow-style kitchen, clients of mine, their space and storage solution was found in the same place.

One of the biggest challenges they faced in their renovation was finding room for a new, 3-ft.-wide SubZero refrigerator. After exploring a few different options for location, I hit on the idea of putting the refrigerator in an old storage closet, which was located across from the new island. The closet entryway was modified so that it would accommodate the refrigerator, making it appear as just another door in the wall.

Behind the new refrigerator, roughly 2 ft. of old closet space remained. Instead of allowing this valuable space to go to waste, I created a bank of deep, pull-out storage drawers for linen and other kitchen items in the butler's pantry located immediately adjacent to the kitchen. The drawers were larger and deeper at the bottom, getting progressively smaller. The fronts were finished to look like those found in many turn-of-the-20th-century kitchens and blended with other cabinetry in the butler's pantry.

Not only did the owners find a home for their new refrigerator that did not take any space away from the new kitchen layout but also discovered a unique and functional storage nook.

(below) Conveniently located beneath the pass-through between kitchen and dining room, a built-in wine refrigerator features wood trim on its shelves that helps it blend with the cherry cabinetry.

Wine refrigerators are no longer just for upscale kitchens. Although they can be placed anywhere, the kitchen or pantry is the obvious spot for keeping wine at hand for meals and parties. (These need not store only wine; they are also great for keeping juices and soft drinks for kids.) The fronts of these units are usually glass. So if you have struggled to hide your appliances behind paneled doors, then you might want to locate a wine refrigerator in a pantry or an adjacent room to the kitchen where it won't be seen.

Dishwashers

Perhaps surprisingly, the original Bungalow era saw a multitude of dishwashing devices, most of which were used in deep sink basins. The built-in style we use now fits neatly into lower cabinetry, and more and more dishwashers have their controls blind-mounted on the inside top edge of the door. This feature, along with the capacity to accept a custom wood panel, ensures that this is one appliance that is pretty easy to hide.

Tucked discreetly within a dark-stained oak cabinet, a wine refrigerator features tinted glass on the front that not only prevents ultraviolet rays from damaging the wine but also helps to blend the modern appliance with the traditional cabinetry.

(facing page) In the Bungalow style, an ultramodern refrigerator can be tied in to the rest of the kitchen through the creative use of woodwork and trim. Here, a built-in refrigerator-and-freezer combination with stainless-steel panels looks right at home.

Still, if you are going with a suite of stainless-steel appliances, it might make sense to choose a stainless panel front to work with the rest of your pieces.

Another new development is dishwasher double-drawer units, which function in similar fashion to the refrigerator drawers discussed earlier. These units also can be fitted with wood drawer fronts so that they look just like regular cabinet drawers, right down to the hardware. If you are going for the concealed approach to your appliances, this is something you'll want to consider. Another nice feature of these appliances is that they can be used more frequently for smaller loads, rather than letting food calcify on dishes in a larger machine while waiting for a full load.

Dishwashers always want to be by your clean-up sink and so can be located either in a run of cabinetry against a wall or in an island, if that's where your sink is located.

An ingenious panel that looks like a drawer over a cupboard door, complete with hardware, hides a state-of-the-art dishwasher. The controls are located on the top inside edge of the door.

This pair of dishwasher drawers couldn't be more modern, but their white fronts against the strong color of the painted cabinets have a decidedly traditional feeling and match the room's white trim.

The black front of a built-in microwave oven relates particularly well to the rich quartersawn cherry of the cabinetry in a new Bungalow kitchen. The dark hardware also helps integrate this contemporary appliance into a more historical setting.

Microwave Ovens and Other Gadgets

Microwaves have become a staple kitchen appliance and need special consideration when they are situated in a Bungalow kitchen. Some people choose to locate their microwave in a pantry or storage area adjacent to their kitchens, but microwaves get used frequently, so shoving them off into another room behind a closed door is not always a practical solution.

Building a microwave into your cabinetry, just as you would build a refrigerator, can solve many problems. The woodwork will tie it in with the rest of the kitchen. Also, it can be positioned to suit your needs, whether that is having the microwave at eye level or, as is increasingly popular, down low, in the lower cabinetry.

Sitting in its own custom-built oak cabinet, this microwave oven blends beautifully with the rest of the kitchen's dark cabinetry as well as with the kitchen's other stainless-steel appliances.

Above this built-in oven is a row of cherry doors, part of a useful appliance garage, which is great for hiding those contemporary gadgets that never look at home on the counter of a Bungalow-style kitchen.

WHERE'S THE MICROWAVE?

The microwave, which for decades has been the elephant on the counter, can be discreetly hidden as part of the cabinetry. Better yet, when installed as part of the upper cabinetry, it is conveniently situated at eye level.

This location solves the problem of being able to see what's going on in the oven without stooping. The slide-out shelf solves the problem of where to put a bowl or dish when loading and unloading the microwave. It all fits into the stained oak cabinetry of this renovated Bungalow kitchen in convincing fashion: The stainless-steel finish of the microwave relates well to the same finish on the refrigerator, immediately to the right.

Another concept is to locate the microwave behind a cabinet door so that it is truly hidden from view. Often this approach includes hiding not only the microwave but also the food processor, the blender, and the waffle iron. These cabinets, known as "appliance garages," are useful for hiding various countertop appliances for a cleaner, more spacious look.

Sinks

A sink is one fixture that hasn't changed an awful lot since indoor plumbing came into popularity in the 19th century. In fact, sinks are one of the few items in a Bungalow kitchen that can be antique—or antique looking—and still do their job perfectly well.

Many variations on the trusty kitchen sink are available today. They tend to fall into one of three types: sinks that sit on top of a counter (top mount), hang underneath the counter (undermount), or are freestanding pieces with their own legs. Top-mount sinks work well with counter materials that are either sensitive to water, like wood, or uneven, like tile.

A detail of the flush-mounted farmer's sink shows how the tile of the countertop snuggles up against the edges of the sink to make a watertight seal, aided by a little flexible caulk. The rounded edges of the sink work well with the bull-nosed counter tile.

These sinks can have an antique, Bungalow-appropriate look when done in enameled cast iron. The heavy rolled top and soft edges of the sink are reminiscent of the old freestanding sinks popular in the early 20th century. This type of sink also works well in a tiled countertop, where the heavy rolled top edge of the sink gives the tile something to edge up against.

Old-Fashioned Basins

The white enameled, double-basin cast-iron sinks on legs that were popular in the original Bungalow years can look great in a new kitchen design. Cast-iron sinks usually included two basins, with one being very deep for cleaning large pots and pans. (Early electric dishwashing devices were often made to fit into this deeper basin.) A sink like this reads almost like a piece of furniture and can be a striking companion to an antique freestanding stove. Most of these sinks have a drainboard area in addition to the sink basins, which if not used for drying dishes, provides a handy counter surface.

Smooth stone counters are well suited for undermount kitchen sinks. The benefit of this is that if the sink basin is attached underneath the surface of the counter then there is no lip on the sink to catch crumbs. Most of the undermount-style sinks are stainless steel, where the smooth face of the sink makes a tight seal with a stone counter. It's hard to get irregular sinks to fit tightly to the underside of a smooth stone slab counter, and as a consequence, an undermount sink has a more contemporary appearance than may be desirable for your Bungalow kitchen.

This hefty porcelain double farmer's sink, or apron sink, nestles comfortably in a tiled countertop. The apron along the front of the sink protects the cabinetry below from water and abrasion. This style of sink was popular throughout the Victorian era but works well within the Bungalow style.

Smooth stone slab provides a good surface for a stainless-steel undermount sink, which is attached to the underside of the stone. The sink cutout in the counter is polished smooth and makes a seamless transition into the sink basin.

A rich blending of materials and colors is at the heart of the new Bungalow kitchen. Here, the handsome wood-plank counter coupled with simple cream-colored cabinetry set next to the pristine porcelain sink feels at once traditional yet modern.

COMING UP FOR AIR

Undeniably convenient for clean-up purposes, undermount sinks present a clean appearance. This historic precedent is found in the Victorian-era wash stands and early ceramic sink bowls mounted under marble tops. They work especially well as part of a kitchen island.

If you decide to install an undermount sink in a wood counter, the edges of the sink cut-out need special attention. The hole exposes the cut ends of the wood grain, which are tiny capillaries. If the grain is not sealed properly, water can be quickly drawn into the wood, causing it to discolor and swell.

The best way to handle this situation is to have the counter installer seal the wood grain in the sink cutout with liquid epoxy. The epoxy soaks deeply into the wood and permanently seals it. This must be done carefully though, so that the epoxy does not discolor the countertop.

Farmer's sinks are popular these days and have an interesting period appearance that works well in a Bungalow setting. Most of these sinks are white, which was the basic color of all plumbing fixtures 100 years ago. If you choose to use one of these sinks in your kitchen, there is an instant simulation of age and a reference to the early years of Bungalow kitchens. Sinks like these might originally have been built to sit on an open stand, or set of legs, but they look suitably retro when built into a run of cabinetry.

Antique or newly built soapstone or slate sinks are an easy way to enhance the antique look of a Bungalow kitchen and have a utilitarian appearance that fits right into the Arts and Crafts aesthetic. These sinks were often found in the basements of Victorian-era homes and were used for laundry and rougher clean-up tasks. They can take a lot of abuse. Slabs of soapstone that are glued together, these sinks don't do well when moved from their original locations. If you find one in a salvage yard, or are bringing one up from the basement, you'll most likely have to reglue the pieces together to achieve a watertight seal. Silicone adhesive works well for this purpose.

Smaller sinks can be handy when located in a prep area of the kitchen or in an island. They aren't large enough to handle most clean-up tasks, but as a source of water for drinks or for rinsing vegetables, you might want to consider locating one of these where it would be effective for you.

This double-basin soapstone sink is an antique, typical of kitchen sinks in late 19th-century farmhouses and early 20th-century Bungalows. Note that the basin on the left is deeper than the one on the right, allowing room for washing larger pots and pans. The twin sinks sit comfortably with the double dishwasher because the rest of the kitchen elements are so light and modern.

The handy bar sink in this marble-countered island is the modern equivalent of pantry sinks in early 20th-century Bungalows.

BUILDING A BETTER REPRODUCTION

As someone who has handled an awful lot of old plumbing fixtures, I can tell you that the new ones not only look old but are operated with ease. Sometimes it's worth rebuilding old faucets to get an antique look in your kitchen, but the new ones work so well that unless you are going for as period a look as possible, you may want to choose a new faucet that has an antique look to it rather than suffer with the shortcomings of an old one.

I find that one large basin is more useful than two smaller ones. The two-basin system is a holdover from the days of washing dishes in the sink, where one basin was for soapy water and the other was for rinsing. Since most of us use dishwashers now, one large, single bowl for your sink will provide much more flexibility for your kitchen chores.

Faucets

For a Bungalow kitchen, faucets fall into one of three basic categories: antique faucets; new faucets that are made to look old; and modern types that can be highly functional but have no pretense about any kind of traditional styling.

The more you push the look of your kitchen toward a historical style, the more appropriate the use of an antique or antique-looking faucet will be. The old ones used rubber washers and a greasy string called oakum to keep the water from leaking out of the stop or handle levers. These faucets will begin to ooze water after a while, requiring periodic replacement of the washers and the oakum. If you are willing to put up with this, then there are lots of great-looking faucets that can be had at antique plumbing places or architectural salvage yards.

Newly constructed faucets with traditional styling are probably the best choice for Bungalow-style kitchens. The better versions use a ceramic valve to stop water flow, and these don't drip or need attention the way their antique counterparts do.

One of a pair of retro-style chrome-plated faucets installed in a double-basin soapstone sink, this faucet has an old-fashioned utilitarian appearance, enhanced by the integrated soap dish, a common element in faucets in early Bungalow kitchens.

In the early days of indoor plumbing, hot and cold faucets were separate pieces and didn't blend the two temperatures the way new ones do. Many of the newly constructed kitchen faucets will have separate hot and cold handles to capture the classic appearance of the old ones even though they blend hot and cold water below the counter.

Another variation is the single-lever kitchen faucet that blends hot and cold through a single spout and just one lever. This single lever can be appealing when you only have an elbow available to turn the water on and off. Most of these single-lever models have a contemporary appearance, but there are versions available that possess antique styling and finish. Once you depart from the simple two cross handles and single-spout versions and begin to add pull-out sprayers, instant hot spouts, and soap dispensers, you'll have to make a decision about whether to go for the "faux antique" look or just let contemporary function express itself for what it is.

An antiqued brass finish was commonplace in an early Bungalow kitchen, and this one's old style adds to the elegant renovation.

A faucet set with all its accessories. From left to right: a soap dispenser, a sprayer, the primary faucet set, and an instant hot tap. All of these pieces have an antiqued brass finish.

STRAIGHT TO THE SOURCE

A swivel-joint faucet is a low-tech solution that presents a utilitarian and Bungalow-friendly appearance. When shopping for fixtures and appliances, it's easy to get lulled into shopping in convenient locations and then being presented with a conventional group of choices. Unique and interesting items can be found in other places, some rather surprising.

For example, commercial plumbing suppliers or janitorial catalogs offer a whole set of options for fixtures that are less centered on trendy appearances and more on function and durability. A rugged appearance can make a faucet or other element look almost antique, perfect for use in a Bungalow kitchen.

Finishes

Finish is an important consideration in a faucet and is often related to the finish of your other kitchen hardware. Keeping your metal finishes uniform is the best design philosophy. Bright polished brass never looks quite right in a Bungalow kitchen. If you lean toward brass as a finish, let it build a patina naturally or purchase it in an antique matte finish, which is more in keeping with the Bungalow look. In the days before brass fixtures were lacquered, they were polished almost daily to maintain their shine. The honest, handmade look of the Bungalow style will work better with darker brass finishes. Otherwise, go for the casual look of nickel finishes.

This "antique" single-lever faucet never exsisted in a Bungalow kitchen. Highly utilitarian, it has a strong sense of majesty and style.

Wall vs. deck mounting

Depending on your counter and sink setup, your faucet will either be wall mounted or deck mounted. The wall-mounted versions have a period look to them, but be careful to add extra insulation if your pipes are located in an exterior wall. Plumbing pipes for the deck-mounted faucets run up through the counter surface or through the back of the sink itself, which allows the piping to run up inside the lower cabinet base and keeps the pipes out of the exterior wall. This kind of consideration is important in cold climates and is easily overlooked in the construction process.

Chrome will work too but can appear too slick and modern in a Bungalow kitchen. Real nickel finish allows some of the brass of the fixture underneath to show through, giving it a slightly yellowed or warmer look that is subtle and beautiful, particularly when blended with other Bungalow styling.

When planning the working elements of your Bungalow kitchen, keep the balance of period-style and modern technology in mind. Achieving this mix is the key to the new Bungalow style.

Old-fashioned gadgets like this nickel-plated ice crusher, here located in a wet bar area, blend perfectly with more hand-hewn elements of the Bungalow style.

6 | FINISHING TOUCHES: LIGHTING, HARDWARE, AND CLIMATE CONTROL

There's an old adage that goes something like this: "God is in the details." That thought definitely holds true when planning and creating a Bungalow-style kitchen today. The finishing touches—the lighting fixtures, the hardware on the cabinets and doors, and even the registers (old or new) over the heating and cooling ducts—can make strong statements and may even serve as defining elements in a new kitchen.

Reproductions of early 20th-century chandeliers, pendant lamps hang over the island in a Bungalow kitchen, providing the main decorative lighting feature for the room. The Arts and Crafts-style fixtures appear hand-wrought, especially the metal banding that supports the dark amber mica glass of the shades, which proudly reveals the rivet fasteners that hold the bands together. The chains from which the fixtures hang are typical of original Bungalow-era lighting.

A pendant lamp hangs over a breakfast table in the informal dining area of a Bungalow kitchen. Although the lamp is a contemporary piece, its simplicity and functionality fit the Bungalow aesthetic. Choices for lighting like this one push the envelope of what is "appropriate" in a new Bungalow kitchen. Unless you want your kitchen to be a literal interpretation of the style, choose lighting fixtures that stay true to the essence of the Bungalow while having a more contemporary appearance.

At first glance, none of these elements seems powerful and certainly not in comparison with other important kitchen components such as the cabinetry or the appliances. Light fixtures are usually relatively small and in some cases are designed to disappear, perhaps literally, into the woodwork.

Heating and air-conditioning are definitely behind-the-scenes players, but these systems need to be accounted for when planning a new kitchen because radiators, grills, and registers need to be sensitively located in your kitchen so that both work effectively and they don't attract

In original Bungalows, shower lights are often grouped along the same beam to produce the most effective illumination.

Published in The Craftsman, July, 1906.

OLD NEWS

Many manufacturers make reproductions of Bungalow-style light fixtures, so many good choices are available, but nothing makes a stronger statement than a beautiful antique. Within the Arts and Crafts lexicon, lots of antique lighting fixtures are easy to find and can be rewired to contemporary standards for use in a new space.

It can be a problem to find the quantities of antique pieces you might need. The best solution: Choose an antique ceiling pendant as the primary focus of the room and then find reproduction pieces to take care of the rest of your needs. This way, when you need to repair or add, you are more likely to find what you need.

THE CRAFTSMAN'S STORY

Some Craftsman Lanterns

Sideboard.

unwanted attention to themselves. Hardware is essential to the finishing touch as well. Like jewelry or shoes, when hardware is of the highest quality, it says a lot about the owner.

Lighting

Think of your kitchen like a stage set. With various lighting options, different scenes can be created according to the activities that take place there. The choices for kitchen lighting fixtures can be broken down into two basic categories: decorative and functional. However, the truth is a well-designed Bungalow-style kitchen needs to have both sorts of lighting to create a satisfying environment. Early Bungalow kitchens were designed with careful attention to windows (often including a window in a heavy exterior kitchen door) so that sufficient daylight could flood into the kitchen. Also, because electrical lighting was in its infancy and gas fixtures did not emit a great deal of light, the level of artificial light in the kitchen (and, indeed, in all the rooms of the house) was much lower than what we have come to expect today. Although the lighting fixtures were often beautiful, they didn't put out a great deal of light by contemporary standards.

The trick with lighting a Bungalow kitchen is to get the levels of light we require but maintain a traditional appearance overall. This may require some sleight of hand. Historic-looking fixtures should predominate, but other contemporary lighting devices need to come into play to augment the light. At no point, however, should supplemental lighting be obvious. This may sound difficult, but if you follow the information in this chapter, you will find the right mix.

Decorative Light Fixtures

Decorative fixtures come in a variety of forms: ceiling-mounted lights; ceiling-mounted lights with hanging pendants; wall-mounted fixtures (sconces); table lamps; and floor lamps. Each of these styles has its historic precedents, including in the original Bungalow era.

The decorative flavor of the Arts and Crafts of Bungalow style featured lighting fixtures with art glass combined with some sort of metal hardware, including wrought iron, brass, or bronze. Cage or square lantern-style lamps with art-glass diffusion panels were seen in pendant versions, as well as bracketed for use as interior and exterior sconces.

These fixtures, which were often hung as pendants on matching chains as with other hardware, were very hand-hewn looking and were often made of dark brass. Typically they were combined mica or other art-glass shades and cast a warm glow over the room.

Other pendant lights were much simpler, featuring little more than a fitter, or brass ring, that would hang from a chain or cloth-covered wire from the ceiling. Glass shades in an infinite array of sizes, colors, and styles were designed for this universal fitter so homeowners could choose specific patterns to suit their taste.

Shades. Milk glass was frequently used during the Bungalow era to create shades for light fixtures. This thick glass softened the glare of electric light bulbs. Shades made of white milk glass were often used in public buildings such as hospitals, post offices, and schools. Today schoolhouse-style light fixtures are often reproduced and work well as pendant lamps in new Bungalow kitchens.

BUNGALOW STYLE

SEARCHLIGHTS

One period-style lighting fixture design that works beautifully today is the holophane light shade. The ribbed glass has a prismatic effect that both amplifies and diffuses the light from the bulb, much the way a lighthouse casts light. The originals, commonly produced in the early 20th century, were generally used in stores, factories, and other commercial venues, making them a natural choice for a Bungalow-style kitchen today. Reproductions are easy to find.

As lighting design progressed into the 1920s and '30s, the fixtures became sleeker, and ceiling-mounted versions, with the bulbs close to the ceiling, not pendant style, began to appear with any number of shade styles. Since ceiling-mounted fixtures introduce a more diffused light into a room, they were often placed in the center of the ceiling, particularly a kitchen ceiling.

On the ceiling. Today, the ceiling-mounted fixture is a perfect choice for a Bungalow-style kitchen, whether it is a pendant-style fixture or one fitted close to the ceiling. Many of today's Bungalow kitchens feature multiple ceiling fixtures, arranged in a line over a peninsula, island, or sink. They can be arranged to give direct light over a particular work area or diffuse light over the entire kitchen. Also, either singly or grouped, they create a stunning effect.

A reproduction ceiling fixture faithfully represents one style that was popular during the Bungalow era. The square, frosted glass shades are a common Arts and Crafts pattern that together with the dark brass fitters and short chains create a strong single light source. The short chains keep the shades close to the white ceiling, which helps to cast the light throughout the room.

Although technically the pendant (one of three that hang over the sink area of a renovated Bungalow kitchen) is a reproduction, it has been designed to be historically true. The cord that the light hangs from is covered in dark brown fabric (before plastic shielding, exposed wires for lighting fixtures were protected this way), and the molded milk-glass shade is one of many choices that would have worked on the fitter, which is the round, dark brass bracket that holds the shade. The shade does a good job of diffusing the light from the 60-watt bulbs inside. The pendant is positioned lower than normal, bringing the light closer to the sink and counter where it is most needed.

This wall sconce is a new piece, but it has enough historic style to feel at home in a Bungalow kitchen. The sconce is one of three that direct task light over the sink and flanking counter.

On the wall. Sconces are light fixtures that are wall mounted and often consist of a single bulb and shade, although many Arts and Crafts versions came with two, three, or more lights. Wall sconces have a number of applications in a Bungalow kitchen. They can light the entry to the kitchen when located just above eye level on either side of the doorway. They can effectively illuminate task areas in the kitchen when mounted at about eye level. Or when placed high on a wall, they work well over sink areas, providing an alternative to pendant lights. Sconces can also work as a decorative element on the walls of your kitchen. The fixtures themselves can be beautiful, and including them in your walls is another way to sneak some more light into the kitchen in an unobtrusive and period-appropriate way.

It is possible to create adequate levels of light in your new kitchen without the use of supplemental "modern" fixtures like recessed lights; it just takes more of the old-style fixtures to do it. This requires a balancing act of sorts because you probably don't want to create a forest of hanging lights from your ceiling or have walls bristling with sconces. Try for a combination of smaller fixtures where general lighting is needed, and save the larger ones to enhance areas like islands, informal dining tables, or other featured spots in your kitchen.

Shedding Some Light on the Subject

Adding an authentic item like an antique pendant lamp or chandelier to a Bungalow kitchen creates a dramatic focal point that instantly conveys a period style. Many well-designed reproduction lighting pieces are available today that look close enough, but when possible, you should always try to find something from the era. An exceptional antique light fixture can add that piece of drama that makes a satisfying difference.

The early electric fixture pictured on the facing page is unique. It was purchased by the owner in an antique shop. In bad shape, it lacked shades and had loose, disjointed parts. A quality lighting workshop replaced all the electric cording and pulled it back together. Then it was suspended from a clever original counterweight mechanism that permits it to move up and down with little effort. The sliding horizontal hardware allows the space between the lamps to be adjusted to accommodate a variety of tasks. The overall effect is historic, functional, and striking.

Although the fixture is not precisely out of the Bungalow lighting canon, its functional appearance allows it to fit in well with the style. The fixture is positioned over the kitchen's center island and is the primary lighting focus of the room. Additional recessed lighting provides more light to the work area of the island. However, because the pendant is so visually captivating, the humble recessed light quickly fades into the background.

Just as with an antique appliance, safety in an old lighting fixture is critical. Many workshops specialize in replacing the wiring in old fixtures, making them completely safe for contemporary use. Good shops can even electrify fixtures that were never done that way in the first place.

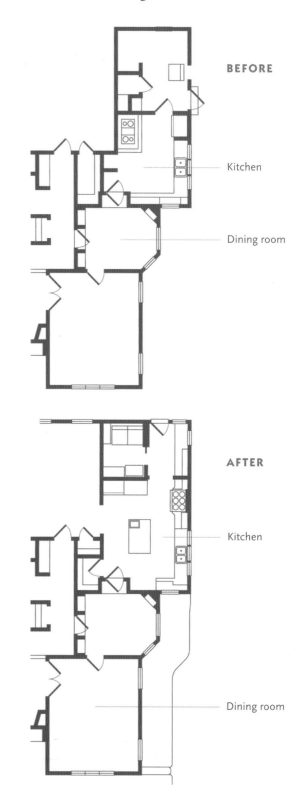

BEFORE

Kitchen

Dining room

AFTER

Kitchen

Dining room

Creating the right balance of functional and decorative lighting can give a Bungalow kitchen an appropriately historical appearance while providing enough light. The decorative pendant and sconce fixtures here capture our attention, while the supplemental recessed lights tend to recede. Under-cabinet lights and the lights in the vent hood over the range can be separately switched on or off to create different moods or to accommodate particular tasks.

BUNGALOW STYLE

Functional Lighting

There are a number of ways to add more light to the kitchen, once the decorative fixtures are placed. Recessed lighting, or fixtures that fit flush in the ceiling, are one choice. As long as there is some kind of other period-looking fixture in the ceiling, then recessed lights can be added to bring in direct light to work areas and pathways without attracting too much attention to themselves. The recessed lights direct their light down, but their light reflects back up too, so the general level of illumination in the room is increased by their presence. Try for the minimum with the recessed lights; too many will overwhelm even the most pronounced decorative ceiling fixtures.

Under-cabinets lights. Under-cabinet lights are sources of light that can be hidden from view under the upper cabinets. The light is directed down at the counter, which both illuminates a workspace and adds more reflected light to the room. These fixtures are available in a number of configurations, but the halogen style produces a white light that makes counters look their best.

Vent-hood lighting. Lighting in a vent hood over the range is another source that can work together with the under-cabinet lights or on its own. Art lighting is another way to get more light into the room, which can be done as either dedicated recessed light or the gallery style of clip-on fixture. Both ways will illuminate the art and reflect light back into the room, helping to bring the overall level up.

THINKING OUT OF THE BOX

An interesting and attractive solution for lighting for a new Bungalow kitchen is a contemporary fixture that is both decorative and functional.

The wood-plank ceiling in this Bungalow-style kitchen is the underside of the finished floors in the rooms above. Such a ceiling does not allow for space to run wires for ceiling-mounted fixtures or pendants. Instead, the owners decided to use halogen light heads on thin decorative wires suspended from the ceiling.

The lights are small enough so as not to call attention to themselves, although their overall effect is theatrical. This suits the owners just fine because their kitchen is located in the center of the other first-floor rooms and is often the main stage when meals are being prepared.

Mounting a small halogen light inside a soffit of an upper cabinet is an effective way to get more light into a kitchen, while at the same time creating a dramatic visual effect. The upper cabinet sits above a peninsula and is visible from the kitchen and the adjacent dining room. Glass doors on both sides of the cabinet allow the light to spill into the rooms, as well as showcase the glassware in the cabinet. Techniques like this are a clever way of introducing more light.

By combining decorative and functional lighting, you will have created a number of possible scenarios for raising the level of light in your kitchen. Particularly if you go the route of dark-stained cabinetry and rich earth tones on the walls, you will need more artificial light to keep the room from feeling too dark and heavy.

If the lights are grouped according to function, you will have the opportunity either to have all of them on at once or create different room settings. The owner of one of the kitchens shown in this book told me that her favorite setting was with just the light in the vent hood on. This she turned on when she came downstairs late at night for a snack. The one light casts a glow that makes the kitchen feel wonderfully cozy and warm.

The lighting design of this restored Bungalow kitchen is simple and provides the amount of light that might originally have been there. Some under-cabinet lighting has been installed, but these lights are used only for task lighting. The three windows over the sink provide lots of daylight and are mirrored by the three hanging pendant lights that align with them.

Windows by the sink bring in a gener-
ous amount of natural light and provide
a lovely view. The period-style pendant
fixture ensures that there is plenty of light
to work by at night.

Creating a Plan

The basic approach I use when laying out the lighting in a Bungalow kitchen is to place primary ceiling fixtures either over an island, an informal dining area, or another feature in the kitchen that deserves highlighting. This helps to create a focus in the room and puts a healthy dose of light where it will be needed.

Supplemental recessed lights can boost this level of light when placed in the ceiling on either side of the larger fixture or fixtures. The featured fixture will be the main focus of the decorative lighting in the room, with the others being subservient. Smaller decorative pendant lights might be located over a sink, work area, or in a breakfast nook. Smaller lights should be in the same or similar design. In this way, none of them threatens to take away the focus from the main fixture or fixtures. Sconces of the same design also can be used with the smaller pendants.

The fixtures need to relate to the cabinetry and furniture in the room so that light is directed where it is needed. When the lighting responds to the functions of the kitchen, an inherent logic that is very satisfying comes into play. This also helps the illusion that all the light in the room is coming from those fixtures. If the period fixtures are located where they make visual sense, add in supplemental fixtures, if necessary, to bring the levels of light up to an acceptable level.

This vignette of an exterior door, window, and back of a built-in breakfast nook bench shows how various hardware pieces work together to enhance the historical feeling of the new Bungalow style. The antique-style metal lock set on the door, the brushed-metal light switch cover, and window pull work together to enhance the style of the kitchen.

Hardware

When we speak of hardware in today's Bungalow kitchen, we are generally referring to the hinges, knobs, pulls, and latches on the kitchen's built-in cabinetry. However, kitchen hardware shows up on a surprising array of items. For example, hardware appears on the windows and doors. Double-hung windows have latches, sash lifts, and various types of stop mechanisms, while casement windows have slides, cranks, hinges, and latches. Doors have hinges, as well as lock sets or passage sets, depending on security or privacy demands.

Switch hitters

Old-style push-button switches with two, three, and four switches are readily available as reproductions, are UL approved, and are safe for use in renovations or new construction. The pearloid-tipped buttons add a touch of elegance, and the metal finishes of the cover plates are a great way to reference other antique hardware. Keeping the metal finishes consistent with other hardware tends to make these devices less visible than conventional plastic switch covers.

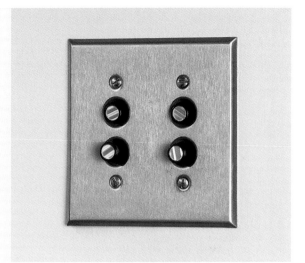

The hardware on lighting fixtures also needs to be taken into account, which includes switch plates and wall socket covers. Even the heating and cooling ducts have registers that are considered hardware.

Cabinetry Hardware

Cabinetry hardware offers an opportunity to make an important contribution to the overall look of your Bungalow kitchen. Many sources are available for period-appropriate Bungalow hardware. Period catalog reprints provide ideas for style, and contemporary hardware catalogs allow you to easily order what you need.

Many excellent reproductions of period designs for cabinetry pulls and knobs are readily available. No single item will carry the style, but remember that with cabinet knobs, the pattern you choose will be repeated over and over again and the cumulative effect is quite persuasive. Also, bear in mind that while contemporary cabinet styles are all about concealed hardware with hinges blinded inside and pulls as low-profile edging on cabinet doors, original Bungalow cabinetry wore its hardware where it could be seen, proudly permitting form to celebrate its function.

A small cabinet latch adds a historic touch to the Bungalow-style oak cabinetry. A mainstay of early 20th-century cabinetry, this nickel-finished latch adds a sparkle of light against the dark wood of the doors. The small turn bolt on the latch is satisfying to operate, always a goal of good hardware.

The Key (and Lock) to an Exceptional Kitchen

As with light fixtures, lots of attractive reproduction hardware pieces are available today, but real antique hardware has a vibe of a bygone era that can add a great deal to a Bungalow kitchen. However, you may face some problems. Finding enough old hardware of the same type to fit out the doors or cabinets in your kitchen may be very difficult. If you live in an original Bungalow, finding hardware that matches what you already have in your house can be harder still. Yet, the solution may be right under your nose.

Many old Bungalows (as well as other house styles of the same period) may have old door hardware on all the doors in the house, including bedroom doors, bathroom doors, and closets. Now, you have a couple of options. You can remove all the doorknobs and escutcheons (cover plates) in, say, the bedrooms for use in the kitchen and replace the borrowed upstairs pieces with attractive reproductions. Or, you can be more subtle and remove the doorknobs from just the inside of the closets, leaving the originals on the outside where they are seen. If you have enough sources for hardware, you can easily make up sets of original hardware to trim out your new kitchen doors. Now you have the matching look you need, and as Laurel and Hardy were known to say: "No one is any the wiser."

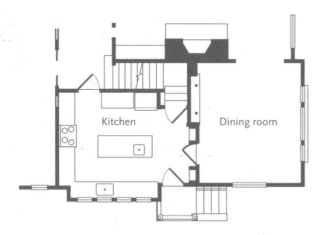

The characteristic patterns for hardware of the Arts and Crafts movement were heavier and more handmade looking (although they were not necessarily made by hand) than today's sleeker, smoothly polished styles. Art Nouveau patterns, Asian influences, and old English styling crept into the designs that were popular in the original Bungalow years.

Hinges. Hinges used in Bungalow-style cabinetry are either "butt" hinges or some variation on what are referred to as "European" hinges. Butt hinges expose their hinge barrel near the top and bottom edges of the door (including cabinet doors) and on most doors are installed in pairs. Taller doors may require more than two hinges. This type of hinge instantly conveys a traditional appearance and looks right at home with Bungalow-style cabinetry.

The easy-to-use drawer and door pulls on this Bungalow cabinetry are reproductions of classic early Bungalow-style hardware. The escutcheons (back plates) show small dimples that evoke a hand-hammered look, while the dark finish and nonrectilinear shape of the escutcheons and the hanging finger loops are common in Arts and Crafts hardware and lighting designs.

The European style, or blinded hinge, does not reveal any of itself on the outside of the cabinet. These hinges are not mounted on the edge of the cabinet door like the butt style, but rather are attached to the inside face (vertical edge) of the door. The benefit of the European-style hinge is that it is adjustable, both up and down and side to side.

Wood cabinets are subject to shrinking and expanding due to seasonal humidity changes, and along with general wear and tear, doors can begin to bind in their openings or show signs of misalignment. Cabinet doors equipped with European-style hinges take only a few minutes with a screwdriver to realign. Butt hinges are more problematic when it comes to adjustment and require considerable skill to manipulate. Also, the fitting of cabinet doors with butt hinges is more time consuming, and as a result, they are almost always more expensive. All this being said, if you want to add an authentic touch to your cabinetry, then butt hinges are the way to go.

BUNGALOW BASICS

New old style

New construction projects provide a blank slate for choosing hardware. It's tough to find old hardware in the quantities necessary for fitting out an entire kitchen, so you'll most likely need to work through reproduction suppliers to obtain your hardware. It can be hard to tell the original pieces from the new ones sometimes, as some manufacturers actually use old pieces to mold and cast the new ones. This is good news. Manufacturers are also aware of the need for suites of hardware, so often a choice you may be drawn to for a door pull will have companion hinges and knobs.

This beautiful little hinge, known as a butt hinge, has a hinge leaf that is quite deep, which allows the window to swing completely in around the depth of the window casing. A shallower hinge would allow the window to only open 90 degrees against the casing. It's a small detail but a defining one.

This original cupboard handle is shiny and wonderfully worn from years of use. Sometimes there is no replacement for the real thing.

An early Bungalow-era passage set design hints at Art Nouveau styling and adds a touch of grace to the door in this Bungalow kitchen. The bright nickel finish works well against the smooth cream-colored paint, while the glass knob adds sparkle and lightness.

Door Hardware

Choosing hardware for a full-size door involves as much time and effort as for cabinet doors. If you are renovating or restoring a kitchen in an original Bungalow, your door hardware should be the same as—or at least consistent with—the hardware on the rest of the doors in the house. When searching out new hardware to match the old, check the new catalogs to see if a reproduction is made of your particular pattern.

Some salvage companies buy hardware and stockpile it. Many companies made cabinet, door, and hinge patterns during the Bungalow period and distributed it nationally. If you are looking for a specific design for, say, a door handle, you might find the same hardware in a Bungalow in Maine as one in California. So, keep your eyes open wherever you go; you may find exactly what you are seeking in a surprising place. In addition, there are specialty manufacturers that still make the old-style hardware for doors. The cost is higher, but the quality is unmistakable.

Window Hardware

Windows, whether double hung or casement style, require a fair amount of hardware. If you are renovating an old Bungalow, as with hardware on doors, try to find new hardware that is the same as or similar to the original. If you are building a new Bungalow kitchen, choose window hardware in traditional style and finish.

Hardware for Light Fixtures

Light fixtures of the Arts and Crafts era leaned strongly on metal craftsmanship and design. Copper, wrought iron, brass, bronze, and tin were frequently used. Pendant lights hung from metal chains, and art-glass globes and lanterns were supported with metal fitters. Again, when choosing light fixtures, check out period catalogs, and choose consistent styles and metal types. This also holds true for switch plates, plug plates, and other pieces associated with light fixtures.

BUNGALOW BASICS

The finish on the finishing touch

Bungalow-style hardware, whether antique or reproduction, is the finishing touch in a Bungalow-style kitchen. When you come to make these choices, make sure the finish on these finishing touches is authentic. Oil-rubbed bronze, antique brass, and satin nickel are good choices. For many Arts and Crafts kitchens, blackened metal is utterly perfect. In any case, it should look like it has been there for decades.

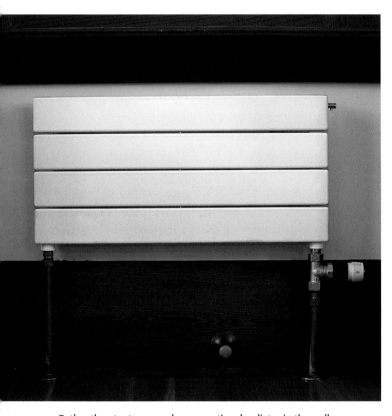

Rather than try to conceal a conventional radiator in the wall or choose an antique-style freestanding radiator to stand off the wall, the architect for this kitchen chose a flat-paneled European-style radiator that sits tight against the wall. The radiator is carefully centered under the window so that it becomes part of the composition. Also, radiators always work better when placed under a window because the cold air from the window creates a circulating convection with the warm air generated by the radiator.

Heating and Air-Conditioning

In the good old days, the cookstove heated the kitchen. Since cooking is an everyday event, the kitchen would always stay warm—even in summer when the extra heat wasn't particularly welcome. Many original Bungalows would have had no other heat source than the cookstove.

Today, we rely on sophisticated heating and cooling systems to keep the kitchen comfortable year-round. Heat comes from either heated water or air, electric baseboards or radiant systems that work with either electricity or circulating hot water. Heating systems that rely on water are called hydronic, and the heat is delivered via steam, circulating hot water, or a hot water coil that is integral to an air-delivered system. Air also can be heated without water in a furnace. A boiler makes either steam or hot water that is circulated through pipes and into various types of radiators.

Air-conditioning must be supplied through either window- or wall-mounted units or through ductwork. However, ducted systems (central air-conditioning) are the least obtrusive and will look the best in a new Bungalow kitchen. If you have a hot-air system, then the air-conditioning can be delivered through the same ductwork. If you have a hydronic system, then you must install ductwork inside the kitchen walls in the course of your construction process.

Register Design

It's important to work with your heating and air-conditioning contractor to choose the most aesthetically pleasing locations for the grills that cover the duct outlets. The contractors will usually go for the locations that are easiest for them to install, but these won't always look good with your carefully planned kitchen. Depending on your system, grills can often be hidden unobtrusively in the toe-kick space of your cabinetry. Standard contemporary grills are made of lightweight metal and make no overtures to the Bungalow style, so you may have to get more creative with this small but important detail.

It's tough to find antique grills and registers that are beautiful and unobtrusive. Heat was created in large furnaces in the basement and rose through ducts that carried the heat up through the house. The early grills were large, were mounted flush in the floor or as boxy devices mounted low in the walls, and could be quite beautiful. However, like other aspects of early Bungalows, the beautifully wrought registers were located in the formal rooms of the house, not the kitchen. Since many original Bungalow kitchens didn't have heat registers, you may be able to find antique registers that match those in the rest of your house at a local salvage yard. For a Bungalow-style kitchen, or if you want to hide the ductwork, go with a simple plate.

The End at the Beginning

With the selection of the finishing—the lighting fixtures, the hardware, and the air-duct covers—the renovation (or original creation) of your Bungalow-style kitchen is complete. You now have nothing left to do except enjoy it!

A well-balanced mix of materials is at the heart of the Bungalow style. Here, the metal heating and air-conditioning register matches the appliances in the kitchen and much of the hardware, giving the whole room a unified appearance.

BUNGALOW BASICS

Electric radiant heating

Early Bungalows rarely had radiators or any other heat source in the kitchen, so they relied on the kitchen cookstove or range to provide the heat. With no original piping or ductwork leading back to the boiler or furnace, providing heat in a renovated kitchen can be tricky. Coils of plastic tubing under the finished floor can supply radiant heat, but this system requires hot water, too. Electric radiant heat can be an attractive solution in situations where boilers or furnaces are too distant from the kitchen or too complicated or expensive to pipe or duct to.

The electric radiant system is composed of heavy plastic sheeting that is installed above the finished ceiling. This system requires that the ceiling cavity be insulated, but if your project requires that the ceiling be replaced, then insulating is not difficult. The radiant panels provide a low-voltage heat that makes the ceiling warm but not hot to the touch. The heat radiates downward and heats objects in the room, not the air itself. A wall thermostat controls the level of heat in the kitchen.

A beautiful copper heat register that is of a type common in houses in the Midwest and West sits proudly in the baseboard of this Bungalow kitchen. Rather than fading in with the woodwork, the piece gives the kitchen a strong sense of historic integrity.

RESOURCES

1. **Barnes Vanze Architects**
Ankie Barnes Principal
1238 Wisconsin Avenue NW
Suite 204
Washington, DC
202-337-7255

General Contractor:
Nuttle Builders of Denton, MD
Cabinets: Browne Architectural
Millwork of Easton, MD
Custom Table: McMartin & Beggins
Furniture Makers
Sink: fireclay sink from Shaw®
Faucet: Rohl®
Cabinet pulls: Whitechapel
Refrigerators: SubZero®
Stove: Viking®
Dishwasher: Asko® model #D1996FI
Under-counter lights:
Seagull® ("Ambiance")
Recessed fixtures: Juno®
Grill/griddle: JennAir®
Vent hood: Viking®
Windows: Marvin®

2. **The Bungalow Company**ᔆᴹ
P.O. Box 584
Bend, OR 97709
541-312-2674

Cabinetry: Matt Gobeille, Harvest
Moon Woodworks, 66224 Barr Road,
Bend, OR, 97701, 541-330-3960
Light fixtures: Schoolhouse pendants,
Dining room: Rejuvenation, Inc.®
Chandelier: Rejuvenation, Inc.
*Recessed fixtures and
under-cabinet lighting:* Juno
Cabinet and door hardware:
Rejuvenation, Inc.
Kitchen equipment, Range: DCS®
Refrigerator: Sears®
Sink: Kohler®
Faucets: Grohe®
Dishwasher: Bosch®
Doors: West Coast Door
Windows: Pozzi®
Breakfast nook:
The Bungalow Company

3. **The Classic Group, Inc.**
420 Bedford Street
Lexington, MA 02420
781-761-1200

Cabinetmaker:
Kochman, Reidt, and Haigh
Light fixtures: Rejuvenation, Inc.
Cabinet hardware:
Crown City Hardware
Range: Antique Magic Chef® (1930's)
Doors and windows: Marvin
Counter stone: Aldrich Stone

4. **Flashback Design**
6336 NE Garfield Avenue
Portland, OR 97211

Cabinetmaker:
Greenline Woodworking,
Patrick O'Neil, Portland, OR
Pendant light fixtures:
Rejuvenation, Inc.
Under cabinet lights: Kichler®
Range: Dacor®
Hood: Vent-A-Hood
Refrigerator: SubZero
Sink: Cessame
Faucet: Chicago Faucet®
Doors: Simpson®
Windows: Marvin

5. Genesis Architecture, LLC
4061 North Main Street,
Racine, WI 53402-3116
262-752-1894

Cabinetmaker:
Kraemer Kitchen Kabinets
Pendant fixture: Forecast®
Recessed fixture: Halo®
Cabinet and door hardware:
Colonial Bronze
Range, oven, and hood: Wolf®
Fridge and wine cooler: SubZero
Microwave: KitchenAid®
Kitchen sink: Whitehaus®
Faucet: Kohler
Dishwasher: Bosch
Doors and windows: Marvin
Counter and island stone:
Brazilian soapstone
Backsplash tile: Motawi Tile

6. Hermannsson Architects
2659 Spring Street,
Redwood City, CA 94063
650-364-8016

General Contractor:
Davey Hubay, owner
Cabinetmaker: husband and wife
team, friends of the owner,
who came over from Germany
Light fixtures: salvaged, Berkeley
Architectural Salvage, Berkeley, CA.
Cabinet hardware: unknown;
Door hardware: Berkeley Architectural
Salvage, Berkeley, CA.
Kitchen equipment: Range and oven,
Wedgewood®; Hood, Thermador®;
Dishwasher, Maytag®; Refrigerator,
SubZero with custom panels; Sink,
enameled cast iron from salvage;
Faucet set, Chicago
Countertop: salvaged crushed glass
set in concrete and ground to a
smooth finish. Custom made by
Counterproductions, Berkeley, CA.
Radiator: Runtal®

7. Johnson Partnership
1212 NE 65th Street
Seattle, WA 98115
206-523-1618

Cabinetmaker: Eastside Millwork
Under-cabinet fixtures are
fluorescents fixtures. Halogen
mini-spots used in soffit above
the west counter are Halo® and the
small recessed lights used to light
the stair to the basement are also
Halo fixtures
Cabinet, door, and window hardware:
Salvaged period hardware was used
for doors and old windows; Häfele®
hardware was used for cabinets
Range: "Bocuse Cooker" made
by Rosieres (Italian-made),
supplied by Professional Home
Kitchens
Hood: Abakka hood (Danish)
with Vent-a-Hood fan
Refrigerator: KitchenAid
Dishwasher: Asea (Swedish)
Sinks: Seattle Restaurant Supply
(large stainless); Ellkay® (small
stainless)
Faucet sets: Chicago Faucet
Counter stone: verde giada marble
from Northwest Marble.
Backsplash tiles: white "subway" tiles
from Art Tile in Seattle.
Linoleum floor: Forbo®

8. Johnson Partnership
1212 NE 65th Street
Seattle, WA 98115
206-523-1618

Cabinetmaker: Cornerstone Cabinets
Low-voltage lights: li'l Wok
by Tech Lighting℠
Recessed lights: uno
Cabinet hardware:
Rocky Mountain Hardware
Range: Wolf
Hood: Vent-a-hood
Dishwasher: Miele®
Refrigerator: GE Profile®
Sink: Kohler
Faucets: Chicago Faucets
Counter and island stone: Soapstone.
Backsplash tile: Custom design from
Heath Tile in Sausalito, CA
Linoleum floor: Forbo
Light switches and switch plate covers:
Rejuvenation, Inc.
Toe-space heat register cover grill:
Restoration Hardware℠
Pot rack: Enclume® from Sur La
Table℠

9. Johnson Partnership
1212 NE 65th Street
Seattle, WA 98115
206-523-1618

Cabinetmaker: Rand Piggot,
Grandworks

Cabinet glass: Seattle Art Glass

Lighting: Rejuvenation, Inc.

Counter material: Stainless steel
by Ballard Sheet Metal

Island stone: Honed granite
by Tile and Stoneworks

Backsplash tile: Emerald Tile
and Design

10. Brantley Ellzey
1166 Overton Park
Memphis, TN 38112
901-274-4455
www.brantleyellzey.com

General contractor/carpenter:
Jon M. Meredith

Cabinetmaker: Advance
Manufacturing (base cabinetry)

Light fixtures:
Sconces: Rejuvenation, Inc.

Cabinet and door hardware:
Home Depot®

Range: Thermador

Hood: Venmar SM

Microwave: Kenmore®

Sink: Kohler

Faucet: Vintage

Refrigerator: Frigidaire®

Counter tile: Country Floors WT
Craftsman series by Pratt & Larson

Island surface: Carrara Marble

11. Kajer Architects, Inc.
Georgie Kajer, Architect
with Erika Lanselle
project manager
1210 East Green Street
Pasadena, CA 91106
626-795-6880
www.kajerarchitects.com

Light fixtures: Pendant at island
and reproduction pendants: Antique
fixture through Reborn Antiques,
Los Angeles, CA 310-659-3358;
Under-cabinet lights: Hera® halogen
"Puck" lights

Cabinet and door hardware:
Rejuvenation, Inc., Portland, OR,
888-401-1900

Range top: 36" gas Viking

Hood: custom enclosure,
with Vent-a-Hood insert

Dishwasher: Viking

Refrigerator: 48" Viking

Microwave: Viking

*Under-counter refrigerator
(not a wine refrigerator):* Viking

Sinks: Rohl "Allia" through George's
Pipe & Supply, Pasasdena, CA
(main sink); vegetable sink: Kohler

Faucet sets: Newport Brass®

Counter stone: Carrara Marble
counters with a honed finish

Backsplash tile: Ann Sacks Tile®,
Kibak series, "Camelot,"
Los Angeles, CA

12. Kajer Architects, Inc.
Georgie Kajer, Architect
with Erika Lanselle
project manager
1210 East Green Street
Pasadena, CA 91106
626-795-6880
www.kajerarchitects.com

General contractor: Jim Stuart,
Homecrafters Building Company,
Glendora, CA, 626-824-0708

Cabinetmaker: Custom vertical-grain
Douglas Fir cabinets made by
Jim Stuart and custom finished
by GD Painting, Los Angeles, CA,
323-422-1675

Light Fixtures: Pendants: Hudson
Valley Lighting, through Historic
Lighting, Monrovia, CA
626-303-4899; Recessed lights:
Halo Incandescent downlights;
Under-cabinet Lights: Hera halogen
"Puck" lights

Cabinet hardware: Rejuvenation, Inc.,
Portland, OR

Window hardware: to match existing,
through Royal Window Company®,
Pasadena, CA 626-796-7565

Range: 48" Thermador gas range

Hood: Custom hood by Homecrafters Building Company with Vent-a-Hood

Microwave: KitchenAid

Dishwasher: Miele

Refrigerator: 36" Kenmore

Wine Fridge: GE Monogram®

All sinks: Blanco Sinks®

All faucet sets: Chicago Faucets with metal lever handles

Counter stone: "Golden Oak" granite with a honed finish, through Elite Construction, South Pasadena, CA, 626-862-0155

Backsplash tile: 3x6 "Subway" tile backsplash and 6x6 decorative reproduction Batchelder scenic tiles through Mission Tile West®, South Pasadena, CA, 626-799-4595

New windows: Custom casement windows with seeded glass and wood-frame copper screens through Royal Window Company, Pasadena, CA, 626-796-7565

Doors: T.M. Cobb through Royal Window Company, Pasadena, CA 626-796-7565

13. PROJECT DESIGNER:
Elizabeth Peck Holmes
Peck Design
172 Encinal Avenue
Atherton CA 94027
650 322 6602

CONSULTING ARCHITECT:
Ana Williamson Architect
885 Santa Cruz Ave. D
Menlo Park, CA 94025
650-329-0577

LIGHTING DESIGNER:
Melinda Morrison Lighting
191 Arbor Lane
Moss Beach, CA 94038
(650) 728-2177
Palo Alto, CA 94301

General Contractor: Rob Berret, Berret Construction, 408-371-5755

Cabinetmaker: Frank LoNardo, LoNardo's Woodworking by Design

Light fixtures: Pendants, sconces, under-cabinet, recessed

Cabinet hardware: Restoration Hardware, and Killian Hardware

Range and hood: Viking

Doors and windows: Loewen®

**14. Joe Metzler
of SALA Architects**
424 Oliver Avenue South
Minneapolis, MN
612-379-3037

General contractor: Reuter Construction, Minneapolis, MN, 612-823-3489

Frieze ("Alise"): Bradbury & Bradbury, Benicia, CA, 707-746-1900

Kitchen cabinet hardware: Nob Hill, Minneapolis, MN, 612-824-7424

Switch plates and cabinet knobs/bin pulls: Rocky Mountain Hardware

Door handles: Von Morris Corporation®

Kitchen flooring: Armstrong Marmorette®, 19081 Black (authorized dealers)

Kitchen lights: Filaments, Minneapolis, MN, 612-870-9621 (custom cloth cords by Paul Stafford Electric, Minneapolis)

Ceiling fan: G-Squared, San Luis Obispo, CA, 877-858-5333, Acero Model #F601

Gas range and range hood: Thermador

Range backsplash: Viking

Dishwasher: Bosch

Refrigerator and microwave: Amana®

Convection oven: Dacor

Accent tiles in kitchen backsplash: Poppy Series, Jade from Motawi Tileworks, Ann Arbor, MI, 734-213-0017

Subway tiles in kitchen blacksplash: Custom-made by North Prairie Tileworks, Minneapolis, MN, 612-871-3421

Granite countertop in kitchen: Land of Lakes Tile & Stone, Albertville, MN, 612-497-7333, Tropical Brown, honed to remove sheen

**15. Scholz and Barclay
Architecture**
P.O. Box 1057
Camden, ME 04843
207-236-0777

General contractor: R. A. Lane
Construction, P.O. Box 108, West
Rockport, ME 04865, 207-236-4064

Cabinetmaker: Designed by
architects and built by Edward Ott,
451 Bunker Hill Rd., Warren, ME
04864 207-273-3722

Light fixtures: Entry pendant fixture:
an antique kerosene fixture
purchased at and electrified by Brass
& Friends, Main Street, Hallowell,
ME, 04347, 207-626-3287;
Kitchen halogens: Tech Lighting℠

Kitchen cabinet hardware: Häfele
chrome plated steel handles of the
116 Series of various lengths;

Interior door hinges: Crown City
Hardware #339a steeple topped cast
iron Victorian patterned hinges

Interior door knob sets: Crown City
Hardware # A245b black antique
porcelain knobs with # 92aa-2
cast iron rosettes

Interior pocket door flush pulls:
Crown City Hardware #339h cast iron
Victorian patterned sash lifts

Kitchen pot racks: Concept
Housewares 36" wall mounted
pot rack with shelf in grey with
cast aluminum hooks

*Cast iron hot air registers and return
register:* Reggio Registers®, cast iron,
various sizes

Range: antique cast iron, Victory
Crawford by Walker & Pratt Mfg. Co.,
Boston combination wood-gas
purchased from Erickson's Antique
Stoves, Inc., 2 Taylor St./ Box 2275,
Littleton, MA 01460

Dishwasher: Fisher & Paykel®
#DD602 SS stainless steel double
dish drawer (now the similar number
is called the DD603M)

Refrigerator: SubZero #611 stainless
steel 30" over-under

Sink: Kindred Industries #KSS5U
30.125" x 19.125" x 9" deep stainless
steel undermount sink

Faucet: Moen® #7375C Chrome/
Chrome One Touch with pull-out
spray, deck plate not used

*Counter stone and kitchen area floor
tile and range:* Vermont green slate,
honed finish supplied, cut, and
installed by Coastal Tile, 59 Union St.,
Camden, ME, 40843, 207-230-0585

Floor flooring: Custom-milled poplar,
also by A.E. Sampson, painted

Ceiling beams: Douglas Fir with
oil rubbed finish

Ceiling: stock 2 x 6 V-groove tongue-
and-groove pine with oil-rubbed finish

**16. Kelli Smith
and Brandon Hatfield**
1534 48th Street
Des Moines, IA 50311

Cabinetmaker: Robb Lynch,
Columbia, Missouri

Cabinet Pulls: Square oak pulls
purchased at Woodsmith Store

Range: Premier ProSeries

Hood: Whirlpool® Gold

Microwave: Emerson
Professional Series

Dishwasher: Maytag

Refrigerator: KitchenAid

Faucet: Price Pfister®

17. Stephen Blatt Architects
10 Danforth Street
P.O. Box 583 DTS
Portland, ME 04112-0583
207-761-5911

General Contractor:
Warren-Hall
Construction Group

Cabinetmaker: John Chaplin

Range: DCS

Hood: DCS

Dishwasher: Fisher & Paykel

Refrigerator: SubZero